Cognitive Biases:

A Fascinating Look into Human Psychology and What You Can Do to Avoid Cognitive Dissonance, Improve Your Problem-Solving Skills, and Make Better Decisions

© Copyright 2020

All Rights Reserved. No part of this book may be reproduced in any form without permission in writing from the author. Reviewers may quote brief passages in reviews.

Disclaimer: No part of this publication may be reproduced or transmitted in any form or by any means, mechanical or electronic, including photocopying or recording, or by any information storage and retrieval system, or transmitted by email without permission in writing from the publisher.

While all attempts have been made to verify the information provided in this publication, neither the author nor the publisher assumes any responsibility for errors, omissions or contrary interpretations of the subject matter herein.

This book is for entertainment purposes only. The views expressed are those of the author alone, and should not be taken as expert instruction or commands. The reader is responsible for his or her own actions.

Adherence to all applicable laws and regulations, including international, federal, state and local laws governing professional licensing, business practices, advertising and all other aspects of doing business in the US, Canada, UK or any other jurisdiction is the sole responsibility of the purchaser or reader.

Neither the author nor the publisher assumes any responsibility or liability whatsoever on the behalf of the purchaser or reader of these materials. Any perceived slight of any individual or organization is purely unintentional.

Contents

INTRODUCTION 1
PART 1: PSYCHOLOGY AND THE HUMAN MIND 3
PART 2: COGNITIVE BIASES 19
PART 3: TOOLS FOR THE MIND 39
CONCLUSION 102
RESOURCES 103

Introduction

The human brain is a complex device, and we still don't understand every one of its functions. In this book, we will take a look at a few functions that have to do with biases. You can find them in every corner of society, from the press to television, from the meeting room to the dining room. They have plagued us forever, but we are now starting to comprehend the threats they pose and understand them a little better.

On a more personal level, you can help fight these biases by being less biased. To do so, you need to identify your own biases, which is what I will show you how to do.

Let's be real here. We have all been there before. We had (or still have) poor thinking, decision making, and problem-solving abilities, and we have to clean up after the messes we've made.

But that ends today. Here, I will help you to identify and overcome your own biases and show you some thinking "hacks" to help you be a more effective thinker. It doesn't matter what your current strengths and weaknesses are in life. It does not matter if you let your emotions run free and control every aspect of your life. These things can be fixed, and you can do so without signing up for some complex training program, either.

Just take a moment now and imagine how simple life would be for you if you could just think and make decisions faster and without bias. We all want to be able to learn to do this. Now is the best time to get started.

Part 1: Psychology and the Human Mind

Brain Psychology: How Humans Think

Let's start from the beginning. To understand biases and other funny aspects of the human mind, you need to understand how our minds function. Don't worry. You won't get a dose of Psychology 101 here. We'll just cover basic information to give you a better understanding.

Have you ever wondered why we do things the way we do? Even though we strive to know ourselves, the reality is this—we don't know very much about our minds, and we know even less about how other people think. Charles Dickens once said, "A wonderful fact to reflect upon, that every human creature is constituted to be that profound secret and mystery to every other."

Psychologists have been working hard to study the human mind so they can find out how we see the world around us and understand what drives us into action. The brain is the most complex device, and the fact that something like this exists is a miracle. While the function of a single neuron in the brain can be understood and the general function of neural networks are vaguely grasped, the workings of the brain in its entirety is a mystery. So far, we have come a long way in understanding the brain, although there is still much to be learned. While different people have different mindsets and brain structures, we have learned, through many infamous studies and experiments, a few universal truths concerning human nature. Below are ten of those truths; truths that might just change your understanding of yourself.

Everyone Can Be a Little Bit Evil

Perhaps one of the most infamous experiments in the entire history of psychology is the Stanford prison study that took place in 1971. The study looked at the way human behavior is affected or influenced by social situations; a "prison" was created in the Stanford University psychology building basement by a group of researchers, led by Philip Zimbardo. Twenty-four undergrad students were then selected. None of them had any kind of criminal record, and all were healthy, in psychological terms. The students were to act as prisoners and prison guards, and they were observed by the researchers using hidden cameras.

While the experiment was meant to last for several weeks, it had to be stopped after less than one week. The prison guards were exhibiting extremely abusive behavior, not just physical but psychological torture, too, resulting in the prisoners becoming anxious and emotionally stressed.

Phillip Zimbardo went on record as saying, "The guards escalated their aggression against the prisoners, stripping them naked, putting bags over their heads, and then finally had them engage in increasingly humiliating sexual activities. After six days, I had to end it because it was out of control—I couldn't really go to sleep at night without worrying what the guards could do to the prisoners."

We Rarely See What's Right in Front of Us

Do you think that you know everything going on about you? You might do, but then again, it's more likely that you don't. None of us are every really fully aware. Back in the late 1990s, Kent and Harvard researchers tested people walking through the campus at Cornell University to see how well people noticed their immediate environment. During the test, an actor would go up to a person and ask for directions. As the person was providing those directions, the scientists would send two men with a wooden door who would walk in between the two, cutting them off from each other's view for some seconds. With no visual contact, the actor switched places with another actor, wearing different clothes, different hair, different voice, even with different height and build. About 50% of participants thought that the actor was the same person. They did not notice that they were talking to another actor.

So, what does this tell us? This was one of the original studies to explore the phenomenon called "change blindness." This goes to show that the human race is, on the whole, quite selective about the information they take in from our immediate environment or scene. It appears that we have a lot more reliance on pattern-recognition and memory far more than we realize.

It's Hard to Delay Gratification—But When We Do, We Experience Success

You might have heard of this experiment before. This was known as the famous Stanford marshmallow experiment that took place in the late 1960s. In this experiment, scientists wanted to see how preschool children resisted instant gratification when it was right in front of them. Instant gratification is the modern-day plague that kills off everyone slowly with an empty, unfulfilled life. From this experiment, scientists learned a lot about willpower and self-discipline. They put four-year-old children into an empty room and gave them a plate with a single marshmallow on it. The children were given a choice—eat the marshmallow now or wait for just 15 minutes. If they could wait, there would be two marshmallows.

Of course, we all know the best option would have been to wait and take the two marshmallows. The children knew that as well, and many of them chose to wait. The problem was that many of them could not resist, giving in and eating it before the 15 minutes' mark and forfeited the 2-marshmallow reward. Children who managed to control their urge and wait for the full length of time employed several tactics to avoid looking at the marshmallows—turning away from them, even covering up their eyes, so they didn't give in to temptation. There were a few significant implications of this behavior; those who can delay their gratification were not as likely to be overweight, or be addicted to alcohol or drugs, or even have any other behavioral issues when they grew up. What's more, is that they proved to be more successful in life.

It is Possible to Experience Conflicts in Our Moral Impulses

Do you know how far someone might go to comply with authority and rules when they are asked to hurt others? In 1961, a study conducted by Yale psychologist Stanley Milgram answered this question. You may not like the answer because the internal conflict of harming others against your own personal morals and any obligation you feel in bowing down to authority causes what is known as cognitive dissonance. I will cover it in a later part of this book.

In this study, Milgram was looking to gain information about why Nazi war criminals did what they did during the holocaust. After all, how could someone do something so evil? Were they inherently evil individuals, or were they just victims of their own circumstances?

So, Milgram tested two participants at a time, one being labeled as the "teacher" and the other labeled as the "learner." Next, the teacher was asked to give the learner some questions, and if the learner answered incorrectly, then he or she would get increasingly powerful electrical shocks; the more questions they answered incorrectly, the worse the shocks got. The teacher was in a different room from the learner, so they could not see what was really going on. The learner was not actually subject to electrical shock, though; instead, Milgram just played recordings to simulate painful screaming. The test was to see what the teacher would do when forced to do something against his will. The teachers would request to stop the experiment, but the researchers would encourage them to continue.

The result came, and it showed that up to 65% of the teachers went up to a maximum of 450V shock. Many of them were visibly distressed and uncomfortable.

What does this experiment tell us? For one, it shows the dangers of blind obedience to authoritative figures. However, some argued the results highlight a deep moral conflict, not blind obedience.

Since humans are social animals, we learn to adapt to other humans around us so we can fit in. That means we have a natural tendency to be good to other people in our group. We also developed a tendency to be hostile to those outside our group. So, the moral conflict here occurs because of association. The teacher can empathize with the student being "shocked," but he was on the researcher's side, so he felt the need to continue to administer electrocution even though he did not feel comfortable doing it.

In the end, it does not matter how one interprets the result. The fact is, some would go all the way to administering a 450-volt shock to another human being just because another person with authority told them to.

Power Can Easily Corrupt Us

Three things can create a tyrant: wealth, power, and fame. Some people can suddenly turn bad when they experience one of those. Sometimes, even your colleagues suddenly start to act all high and mighty after a promotion to a higher position. There is a psychological reason behind this sudden shift in behavior.

In 2003, a study was published in a journal called *Psychological Review*. In this study, the participants were students, and they were divided into groups of three. Each group was tasked to write a short paper together. Since this was a group effort, a group leader was needed, and so one of the three took that position. Two out of each group had to write that paper while the third was asked to judge it and work out how much compensation the writers should get. The researchers did not study so much the effect of the amount of money that would be compensated. This was only done to give the third student, the designated boss of the group, the power that befits the position.

While the groups were working, a researcher would occasionally bring a plate containing five cookies into the room. Further observation showed that the final cookie was almost never eaten, which is still a common sight nowadays. Other than that, they also found that the boss in the group was nearly always the person to eat the fourth cookie, and they often did so in a sloppy manner.

Other than that, the boss of each group was also more likely to touch others, sometimes inappropriately, flirt more directly, make riskier choices, and was often the first person to make an offer in negotiations, the first to voice their opinions, et cetera. Basically, when the students were given more power in the group, they became more open, direct, and daring.

We Seek Loyalty from Our Social Groups and Are Drawn to Conflict Easily

We have had two World Wars and countless armed conflicts between states and between smaller social groups throughout human history. Even with so many deaths, you would think that we would have had enough of war for the entirety of human history, right? Not really. The only reason why World War III hasn't started yet is because of Mutual Assured Destruction (MAD), which is a deterrence against nuclear states from just nuking each other. But I'm not going to discuss MAD here. What I want to explore is the reason why we get involved in conflicts so frequently, and then we become friends with each other so soon, as if nothing happened. A social psychology experiment from the 1950s could provide us with an answer to that.

In this study, volunteer boys aged 11 were divided into two groups. One was called the Eagles, and the other was called the Rattlers. They were taken to Robbers Cave State Park in Oklahoma, and the boys were told that they were going to be at summer camp. The two groups were not aware that the other existed, and they each spent the week in a different part of the camp, engaging in fun activities and forming bonds within their respective groups.

Then, the second phase kicked in, and the groups were brought together. The two groups had certain differences, and it did not take long before conflicts started to happen. First, the name-calling started, and then, researchers introduced competitive games that pitted the two groups against each other, which led to more conflicts. In fact, it got so bad that the two groups got to the point where they would not eat together. But that was not the end of it.

The scientists then decided to try and bring the two groups together. First, they introduced fun activities that both groups could enjoy together, which did not work well. Then, they went ahead and had the boys solve problems together, which worked, and the two groups were a little closer at the end.

What do we learn here? Different social groups are more likely to cooperate with one another when they share a common *problem*.

We Need Just One Thing for Happiness

We hear this all the time. In fact, we might have said it to ourselves at some point in our lives. "Oh, if only I had 'X,' then I would be happy forever." In reality, we always want more and more. I'm talking about material possessions, fame, and power. They could never make us happy. There is only one thing that can grant us happiness, and it was the Grant Study at Harvard University that showed us what it was—a study that lasted 75 years!

In this study, researchers enlisted 268 male subjects from Harvard who were undergraduates. The subjects would be followed and observed for the next 75 years, with data from different bits of their lives being collected at regular intervals.

At the end of the study, researchers determined that at the end of the day, the only thing that really matters is love. That's not to say that power, money, and fame are worth nothing; they are worth something, but you don't need them to live—the only key to long-term happiness is love.

George Vaillant was the director of the study, and he said that love has two primary pillars—happiness only comes when you can find love and when you live your life in such a way that you allow love in. This goes a long way toward explaining why some antisocial people or those who choose to live an isolated life are typically unhappy. They do not let themselves interact with others, and that means love cannot find its way into their lives.

What was amazing about this study was one of the 268 subjects. He was considered by the scientists to be the worst out of all of the subjects. He had the lowest future stability rating. In fact, he was so low that he even attempted to commit suicide. But he eventually came through and became one of the happiest people out of all the subjects. How did he make such a recovery? It was love. He spent his life looking for love.

Social Status and Strong Self-Esteem Help Us to Thrive

There's no doubt that success and fame can give our egos a big boost; it's obvious, but there is more to it than that. There is a school of thought that says self-esteem provides longevity; at least, that's what was claimed by the Oscar Winners study.

Researchers studied directors and actors who were recipients of Academy Awards and, in the process, discovered that they lived, on average, four years longer than those who got a nomination but didn't win.

That doesn't tell us an awful lot really; after all, the winners may just have had a healthier lifestyle, or it could just have been nothing more than dumb luck. However, it does provide some correlation with this theory, although we really don't know if being lucky enough to win an Academy Award can add another four years to your life— don't quit your day job just yet!

What we did learn was that social factors have a role to play in longevity. Self-esteem definitely helps to improve health, and although it may sound like nothing more than pseudoscience, it does kind of make sense. What it really boils down to is this—the more happiness we feel, the longer our lives are, and, as we already know, the key to happiness is love.

We Try to Justify Every Experience so It Makes Sense

This comes under something we'll discuss more in part 2— cognitive dissonance—but it is something that any student of Psych 101 class should be familiar with. All humans will naturally try to avoid any psychological conflict between their actions and their thoughts or beliefs, and, for this, we'll look at a study that psychologists Leon Festinger and Merrill Carlsmith carried out in 1959.

Study subjects were asked to do a series of tasks. These were boring tasks, and they were asked to do them for an hour or so. Each subject would then be given $1 or $20 to say that the tasks were interesting when they clearly weren't. Festinger discovered that the subjects paid $1 enjoyed these boring tasks more than those paid the higher amount. You would think it would be the other way around, so why wasn't it?

It turned out that the subjects who were paid $20 felt that the money was justification enough for doing those tasks and, as such, could be more objective. The subjects who were only paid $1 didn't have sufficient justification for being objective. Cognitive dissonance needed reducing, so the subjects had to find some way of justifying how they behaved; they did this by claiming that the tasks were fun to do.

It boils down to this—we tell ourselves lies so that things appear more logical than they actually are.

We Find it Easy to Buy into a Stereotype

We all stereotype to a certain extent, as hard as we try not to, and it can result in coming to unfair conclusions about people, ethnic groups, classes, entire populations even, and that is potentially very harmful. As an example, we'll look at a study carried out by John Bargh, an NYU psychologist.

He conducted experiments on social behavior and how automatic it is, concluding that, very often, we judge other people based entirely on stereotyping, even though we usually do it unconsciously. More often than not, we do nothing to stop ourselves from doing it.

Humans also tend to buy into social stereotypes, particularly for groups that they are not involved in or a part of. Bargh gave a group of study participants some words that were to do with old age, like "wrinkled" and "helpless," asking them to unscramble those words. Another group was given another set of words, not related to age. Of the two groups, the one that worked on the age-related words walked much slower after the test than the other group. He took the experiment a step further, still using two groups of people, with words related to politeness and race—his findings concluded that we unconsciously enforce stereotyping.

According to Bargh, stereotypes are simply categories that have been pushed too far. He also said that, with stereotypes, we tend to take in the qualities of that stereotype, like age, gender, color of the skin, etc., and our minds will automatically respond with labels, such as hostile, weak, strong, friendly, etc. Those labels do not, in any way, reflect on reality and are purely an unconscious response, based on what we think we know.

Brain vs. Mind: Know the Difference

If you don't have a degree in neurobiology, you're forgiven for thinking that the brain and the mind are the same thing. We use the two terms interchangeably, and in most contexts, this is fine. But when one intends to study the complex system of the human mind, one needs to be able to make a distinction between the brain and the mind.

Here's an example. When you stub your toe, what do you say? Most likely, "I stubbed my toe, and it hurts like hell," and not "The pain receptors in my toe light up and send a signal that travels through my leg, up my spine, to my brain to let it know that the toe just had a collision with a foreign object."

The first response is the mind speaking, whereas the brain does the talking for the second response.

Simply put, the mind is synonymous with our thoughts, feelings, memories, and beliefs. The mind is the source of our behaviors. It is formless, but it is very powerful. On the other hand, the brain is physical and is the source of the mind.

When you experience an emotion or have a thought, the brain lights up certain neurons, and the mind interprets those signals to formulate those thoughts or emotions.

But the distinction is still a debate today. While neuroscientists do not object to discussing the mind in casual conversations, many insist that the mind is not real or distinct from the brain. The idea that the mind is an independent entity from the brain is unacceptable. On the other hand, civilians embrace the distinction, as mind training, such as mindfulness and meditation, has been proven to have positive effects on the brain.

Nonetheless, the debate still rages on today, and the outcome will have far-reaching consequences.

For now, you can believe that the "mind" doesn't exist and whatever you think and feel is just a bunch of neurons in your brain lighting up. Alternatively, you can think of the brain as the computer—the hardware—whereas the mind is the software—the software/system—both of which work in conjunction.

Heuristics: How We Make Decisions

Heuristics is nothing more than a mental shortcut, saving us potentially hours of time in making simple decisions. Heuristics allow us to make quick decisions, which is practical, although it does not guarantee to be the optimal, perfect, or even rational decision. It can at least allow us to reach a short-term goal.

Heuristics are often used when finding the best solution to a problem is impractical or outright impossible. They help speed up the process and take away some of the load from making a decision. Heuristics are commonly used in the following situations:

• **Consistency Heuristic** – when situations are responded to in consistent ways.

• **An Educated Guess** – when a conclusion is reached, even without enough information or research. A person considers what they learned in the past and relates it to a current situation, applying what they think they know, even though it may not be correct.

• **Absurdity Heuristic** – an absurd approach to any situation, when a claim is made that is unlikely, and not based on common sense.

- **Common Sense** - applied to problems or situations based on observation; a practical approach allowing a quick decision to be made when the wrong and right answers are clear.
- **Contagion Heuristic** - when a person avoids something he or she believes is not good. An example would be if a product he or she bought is recalled because of a defect; they may then opt to never purchase from that company again, to avoid the same problem arising in the future.
- **Availability Heuristic** - when a situation is judged based on previous situations similar to it, and a person can apply their previous experience to the current situation.
- **Working Backward** - a method of finding a solution to a problem by understanding what the desired solution is and working back to determine how to arrive at the solution. An example would be a maze game—you know you have to get to the center, you just have to work out how to do it, and the easiest way is to work backward from the center.
- **Familiarity Heuristic** - when someone approaches a problem in the same way that they have approached similar problems in the past, to reach a predictable and similar result.
- **Scarcity Heuristic** - when we want something because it is scarce, suggesting that we place a higher value on scarcity or rarity.
- **Rule of Thumb** - a simple, yet broad approach to solving problems, whereby we make an approximate decision or draw an approximate conclusion, with little need for research.
- **Affect Heuristic** - when a quick impression is used to base a solution or decision on. This is often a helpful heuristic, particularly when in a life or death situation; we can make an immediate decision without the need for research, but, if applied to the wrong situation, this heuristic can cause harm.
- **Authority Heuristic** - when a person believes that another person's opinion is true purely because they are a figure in authority. We tend to see this applied more in politics, science, and education.

It is worth pointing out that overreliance on heuristics can lead to fallacy and biases, which I will cover in the next part.

Part 2: Cognitive Biases

What Are Cognitive Biases?

We are going to explore various biases, both conscious and unconscious, in many contexts such as the workplace, the family, and society at large. This is where things get interesting. Understanding and acknowledging that you have biases is the first step to becoming less biased.

Think of cognitive biases as faults in our thinking systems. We tend to think in a logical, objective way. Cognitive biases are the patterns that stray from that norm or rationality. Most of these biases can be reproduced, and therefore confirmed, by research, but there are often controversies about how one should go about classifying or explaining them.

While biases come in many forms, we can categorize them into two main groups known as "cold" or "cognitive" biases and "hot" or "motivational" biases. The former is all about information, such as neglect of probability, distinction bias, or anchoring. It is simply a miscalculation. The latter is more emotionally-driven, such as wishful thinking. What is more important to note is that both hot and cold biases may be present at the same time.

There are many controversies over the interpretation of biases. I will show you later because some believe that they are not irrational; or that they may lead to useful attitudes or behavior. For instance, let's look at leading questions. When getting to know others, people often ask leading questions, which appear to be biased toward confirming their assumptions about the person. Many argue that this kind of confirmation is simply a way to establish a connection with the other person, so it is simply a social skill, which is not bad in any way.

Of course, when one discusses cognitive biases, one cannot overlook the importance of heuristics. Simply put, a heuristic is a mental shortcut that allows us to make quick and efficient decisions. Heuristics help us shorten decision-making time and allow us to go from day to day without having to stop to think about what to do next.

Quick and efficient heuristics can also lead to cognitive biases. After all, just because something works once does not mean that it will work every time. The best example here are jokes or lies. You tell it once, and it might work, but it won't work the second time around. So, if you rely on heuristics too much, you may not see other alternatives that may be better options. Heuristics can also introduce stereotypes and prejudice because we use mental shortcuts to classify and categorize people, thus overlooking the smaller details. We tend to end up generalizing.

What Are Logical Fallacies?

A logical fallacy is a flaw in one's logical arguments that undermines their validity. Certain logical fallacies appear sound, but they are still fallacies, and it is best to keep an eye out for these subtle variants.

Again, because of the variety of structures and applications, fallacies are difficult to classify in a way that satisfies all practitioners. One can classify them based on their structure or content, divided into subcategories, the processes, et cetera. Below are some of the most common fallacies:

1. Straw Man Fallacy: This is one of the most common tactics people employ to win debates. Basically, they will over-simplify or purposely misrepresent or frame your arguments in a way that makes it easier for them to attack. But that does not mean that they fully address your actual argument. They simply create an easier target, a "straw man," which hopefully convinces other people that this accurately represents your argument. The best way to know whether a person is using this approach is when they begin by saying, "So you're saying." The best strategy is to not respond to the attack on the straw man and reiterate what you were saying.

2. Bandwagon Fallacy: Basing the validity and soundness of one's argument on popularity, or a representation of this popularity (four out of five people recommend "X", et cetera.) This is because the argument does not take into consideration whether the population validating it is qualified to do so.

3. Appeal to Authority Fallacy: While appealing to authority is a sound argument in many cases, relying on it too much can be dangerous, especially if the source of authority is trying to validate something outside its expertise. The simplest case here would be to say that the head of the IT department cannot validate an argument related to the finance department.

4. False Dilemma Fallacy: When someone misleadingly presents a complex issue and offers two mutually exclusive options. It's either "A" or "B" and no in-between. The two options are often on extreme ends of the spectrum, thus ignoring all the possibilities in-between that allow for compromises.

5. Hasty Generalization Fallacy: A general conclusion is drawn from a very small sample size. Just because two people in the entire company report higher productivity from meditation does not mean that the company should impose mandatory meditation sessions.

6. Slothful Induction Fallacy: This is the opposite of the previous fallacy. Basically, even with enough evidence that represents the entire population, one does not acknowledge the validity and soundness of the argument.

7. Correlation/Causation Fallacy: Correlation or causation is when two or more things happen in a given situation, and one event has an impact on the other. For instance, hot sunny days cause sunburn and increase the consumption of ice-cream. The cause is the sunny day, and the ice-cream and sunburn both occur because of this. However, one has the correlation/causation fallacy when they incorrectly claim that ice-cream causes sunburn.

8. Anecdotal Evidence Fallacy: Arguing from one's own experience rather than logical evidence, thus taking one possible isolated example as proof and ignoring the overwhelming proof to the contrary. This fallacy is often seen in cases against vaccination.

9. Texas Sharpshooter Fallacy: This comes from a Texan who shot at the wall of his barn and then painted a large target around the nearest grouping of bullet holes. Then he said that this was proof of his marksmanship. Basically, the person cherry-picks data to support their own argument and ignores a plethora of proof that supports the contrary.

10. The Burden of Proof Fallacy: The burden of proof will always rest on those who make a claim. If someone claims that something is true, then they need to prove it. If there's no evidence presented against it, that doesn't mean it's true.

20 Cognitive Biases

In addition to the logical fallacies we've discussed above, here are 20 common cognitive biases that can interfere with your decision-making:

1. Availability Heuristics: Basically, we see the big terrifying events to be more serious than the more common ones. For instance, many people view plane crashes to be something very scary indeed, but they do not take into consideration that more people die in car accidents than plane crashes. It's true that a plane crash can take 300 souls with it, but deadly or serious car crashes occur a lot more often.

2. Halo Effects: Because our brains love consistency, we believe that when we see one quality in a person, we think that the rest should be just as consistent. Looking for contradictions within a person can be tiring, so we use this heuristic, which turns out to be a bias. The best example is this: "The first impression lasts a lifetime." Basically, when you walk into an interview and make a positive first impression straight away, the interviewer will take you more seriously and view you in a good light, thus increasing your chance of landing that job, even if you have some flaws in other areas. Your positive first impression casts a hazy halo of positivity over all other information.

3. Sunk Cost: To sum this up, it's over-commitment. This is the belief that once we have sunk enough time and resources into something, we are less likely to abandon it, even if the project at hand will fail. Instead of cutting our losses and pulling out early, this bias leads us to keep trying even though it's already doomed, resulting in the loss of more time and resources.

4. Survivorship Bias: We all love success stories. We've known many figures that decided to drop out of college and decided to start up their own tech company, which ended up being multi-billionaire corporations. Many of us know that this is a very risky move, yet these success stories tell us that it is possible, and the ROI is enormous, so we are blinded to the actual probabilities. In this case, we see Mark Zuckerberg, Bill Gates, and Steve Jobs being successful as dropouts, but we do not consider countless other dropouts who are struggling from day to day. Of course, you can possibly strike it rich as an entrepreneur, but the chances are very, very slim.

5. Action Bias: The tendency to choose action over inaction in the face of ambiguity even though taking action is counterproductive. This bias can present itself when people have to make decisions while under pressure, such as in a competitive environment.

6. Framing Bias: This occurs when someone is influenced by how the information is presented, but not the information itself. For example, one could represent an economic downturn between the years 2009 and 2011, even though the economy began to improve again then after the global financial crisis.

7. Strategic Misrepresentation: This bias occurs when someone is being too optimistic and underestimates the cost or risk of their decisions. This often occurs when someone is passionate about their innovative ideas and wants to put them forward and get them into action as soon as possible without conducting enough research to test their viability. It's either that or the person fully understands the risks associated with their ideas, but they have decided to go ahead with them anyway because they "know it will work."

8. Ambiguity Bias: This is similar to action bias. Basically, when a person is faced with a lack of information, their default option would be to stick with what they already know. This is usually a good move, especially when the risks outweigh the benefits, but this can also inhibit innovations as it is in their nature to be unknown and risky.

9. Pro-Innovation Bias: This occurs when there is a belief that something new and innovative needs to be adopted by literally everyone in the team, company, social group, or entire populations. The problem here is that since everyone is inherently different, forcing a new and largely untested concept upon them is never a good idea. But this bias makes innovation look like something that is desirable and inherently good so that all the potential negative impacts fade into obscurity. Those with this bias may not see problems such as sexism, elitism, and inequality that could result from their innovative ideas.

10. Status-Quo Bias: Also known as the "fear of change," people with this bias tend to favor the current situation and do nothing about their circumstances; simply, they are afraid that they may lose something, even though sometimes the only thing they'll lose is their chains. This bias can trap people in a detrimental situation and keep them there for the rest of their lives unless they see the errors in their ways and work to get out of there. This bias is especially subtle because it aligns with the fact that our brains love consistency. The best way to spot this bias is when someone refuses to do something simply because "It's not the way we do things around here," rather than offering a valid reason.

11. Feature Positive Bias: This bias is very similar to strategic misrepresentation bias. People with this bias tend to look at what they stand to gain from an option rather than considering what they could lose from it. This can occur due to limited time and resources that prevent them from thinking objectively, so they then develop a tendency to hope for the best.

12. Affinity Bias: The tendency to favor people who are like ourselves. Birds of a feather flock together, after all.

13. Belief Bias: The tendency to believe that one's argument is logical and sound—not because of the supporting evidence, but by relying on one's own beliefs over the truth of the conclusion.

14. Empathy Gap: The tendency to underestimate how emotions play a role in all aspects of life, in either oneself or others.

15. Hard-Easy Effect: The tendency to view one's own ability as adequate when one has to accomplish hard tasks and inadequate when one has to accomplish easy tasks.

16. The Illusion of Control: The tendency to overestimate one's own control over external events.

17. Hot-Hand Fallacy: The tendency to overestimate the chance of success is higher simply because that person or group has been successful (by luck rather than judgment) in the past. If you have studied probability, the chance of flipping a coin and getting heads five times in a row is substantially lower than getting it three times in a row.

18. Self-Serving Bias: This is similar to confirmation bias, which I will get to, because it is the tendency to evaluate ambiguous information in a way that benefits a person's interests. It is also a tendency to claim more responsibility for success than failures.

19. Hindsight Bias: Also known as the "I-knew-it-all-along" effect, is the tendency to see past events as being predictable. While this bias does not display itself during the decision-making process and therefore is harmless at that stage, it does prevent people from acknowledging their mistake, learning from it, and therefore preventing similar problems from happening in the future.

20. Confirmation Bias: Characterized as the tendency to look for or interpret information in such a way that supports one's own arguments or views, while also discrediting other evidence that supports the contrary. This bias is related to cognitive dissonance, which we will discuss in the next chapter.

Unconscious Biases: They're All Around You

To prove that unconscious biases exist, let's do a quick test. Go onto Google and type: CEO. Look at the top results. More often than not, you will see that there are more images of men in suits than women. Now, you may not see what is going on there, and you're forgiven for that. This is why these things are called "unconscious biases." Many people do not notice these small things in life, although they are just as dangerous to our cognition. The fact that I pointed this out may make me look like I'm nitpicking, but hear me out. What you are looking at is sexism in its most subtle form. Small things like images can reinforce certain stereotypes and demonstrate sexism inherent in our society. These small things are known as "unconscious" or "implicit" biases. Many people would not even notice these subtle things unless we were the ones being discriminated against, or if the images otherwise failed to represent us. These hidden biases and stereotypes impact small things such as designs, images. Though small as they are, they still reinforce biases and are, therefore, just as dangerous.

Unconscious bias (also known as implicit bias) only got its name back in 2006. It started out as a study on the unconscious mind. More specifically, the unconscious mental processes that lead to various problems such as discrimination in governmental institutions and the justice system. This field of study does not accept what was once a long-held belief that our behaviors are only influenced by external or explicit factors such as conscious thoughts or beliefs.

You can find examples of unconscious biases everywhere. The neighborhood that you live in, the people you hang out with, and those who you love. It is inevitable, and everyone has it to varying degrees. Developments in neuroscience now show that biases are formed as we grow up, meaning that we start to develop biases from childhood. To make matters worse, these biases are formed and ingrained at the subconscious level, and they are often reinforced through societal and parental conditioning.

Since we gather countless information and our brain needs to process all of that data, it unconsciously develops ways to categorize and format the data into familiar patterns, so it can process all the data effectively. Those familiar patterns are, of course, unconscious biases. No matter how hard we try to avoid it, we do it all the time. Things like gender, ethnicity, disability, sexuality, body size, professions, etc. all influence our initial impression of another person, and this forms the basis of our relationship with them.

As mentioned before, unconscious bias can be found in many places. Below are three main places to be aware of your biases and how you can deal with them.

In the Workplace

Biases in the workplace are pretty common, especially if the company is not so inclusive. Here are some things you can do to combat biases in the workplace:

Pause Before You Speak

The expression "Turn your tongue seven times before speaking," applies here. This isn't because you need to loosen up the tongue so you can speak properly, but rather to give yourself time to think about what you are actually going to say. This is a cure for what is called "foot-in-mouth syndrome."

A lot of people make the mistake of speaking their mind without practicing the care to select their words carefully. This is when the unconscious biases surface because the brain uses the same bias-ridden system to articulate our thoughts. Unless you consciously select your words, then whatever is coming out of your mouth may sound prejudiced or discriminatory.

There was a journalist whose name I shall not mention, although you may know her already. She thought of what seemed to her to be a funny joke and then tweeted it, saying something along the lines of "I'm going to Africa. I'm afraid of getting AIDS. Oh, wait, I'm white." To her, it was an innocent joke, but it ended up ruining her entire career, and everyone ripped her apart on the Internet.

So, before you speak, let alone make a joke, stop and think how others will interpret your own words. More often than not, people will interpret them in the most negative way possible (partly thanks to their own biases).

The rule of thumb here is: "When in doubt, just don't."

Validate Others' Experiences

Everyone has a different past, so they will have their own sets of beliefs, values, behaviors, and experiences. Accept the fact that it is okay to be different. It really doesn't matter if everyone works together to achieve a common goal anyway. Respect differences. In fact, having a diverse group of people on the team may be helpful, because some of them may have unique ideas that may solve the problem at hand.

Stop to Listen

Ask yourself: how often do you ask a question to which you think you already know the answer? The answer is mostly like to be quite often, and if so, you're either a lawyer, very smart, or you have unconscious bias. Again, this is something that people do all the time. Here's another question: how often do you ask for suggestions from other people although you've already made up your mind?

This is quite common in the workplace. In the corporate world, efficiency is highly valued as it keeps production up and costs down. Unfortunately, speedy decisions are often not recommended.

So, the next time that you ask a question, just listen to what others have to say. Ask follow-up questions if you need to. You might learn a thing or two from other people.

Connect with People Who Are Different to You

Make a habit of seeking out ideas from other people before you voice yours, especially if they have a different perspective from yours. You might want to extend the circle of friends you hang out with if possible because if you have been hanging with the same people for a long time, then you won't learn much more from them.

You want to have a circle of friends from various backgrounds. Whenever there is a discussion, allow and encourage other people to voice their opinions first because they may have something good to say. Keep an eye out for the people who usually do not talk much during meetings. I recommend you seek out their advice and opinions. You might be surprised to hear what they have to say.

Demonstrate Your Support

You should back up your beliefs with actions. If you are an advocate for equality and diversity, then you want to support those who are being discriminated against. If you see someone being bullied in the workplace, stand up for them, and do not be afraid to call the other person out for their unacceptable behavior. Make sure you are polite when you tell them about it, though. More often than not, that person may not know that they are discriminatory. Give them the benefit of the doubt. Just make sure to let them know that their behavior is unacceptable.

At Home/in the Family

We live in a society that constantly changes, so children need to learn how to cope. The biggest thing right now is diversity, and children need to learn how to live with people who are inherently different from them.

Since external factors easily influence children, the responsibility lies with you and others around them to teach them everything they need, and that also includes how not to be biased. The only issue here is that children will interact with other people who are also biased, and they can pass their false beliefs to children.

So, in light of all this, what can we do to help children overcome biases? The best way we know so far is by talking to them about the issue and helping them to understand the situation by having them empathize with the victim. Avoiding "the talk" is going to cause many problems down the road because, again, children look for nonverbal cues that we often unconsciously display. By making it clear with them, they will be a lot less likely to develop biases.

In Society

In society at large, biases are everywhere, especially sexism—both implicit and explicit. Take politics, for example. Back in 2008, both Sarah Palin and Hilary Clinton fell victim to misogyny when they ran for Vice President and President, respectively. Both of them were subject to various vicious comments, and most of these run-ins did not have anything to do with their campaigns. This begs the question, would they have been treated differently, had they been men?

Gender bias is also prevalent in the media. Many women say that they are not accurately reflected in the media; such as television, film, advertisements, broadcast news, et cetera. Although the situation is improving, it is not nearly as fast as it should be, and that is probably only because a small percentage of the media decision-makers, those with enough power to approve which content to put up, are female. Right now, some traditional media outlets are improving how they handle bias, although some say that it is not enough, and there are a number of specialized outlets that do a better job.

But it's not just the news media, either. There are also issues with other types of programming, such as mainstream cinema, which has a lack of diversity in its characters and stories and has a notoriously low number of women with spoken lines in most cases.

Thankfully, women's issues are at the forefront of our cultural dialogue, at least in the United States. We have made great progress over the last few decades as advocates continued their efforts in pushing against these longstanding biases. If people stop speaking out, then these problems will persist.

Beating Your Own Biases

If you want to be less biased and a little less prejudiced, then there is good news and bad news. The bad news is that we are naturally biased, because the only way we can make sense of the world is through generalization and putting things and people into mental categories that our minds create on their own. These categories can imply good and bad things. A human with zero bias is a human that just cannot function because they waste a lot of time trying to experience the world from an objective standpoint, making no inferences or assumptions. What does this look like in practice? Not taking a flight because you do not trust the pilot or not assuming that the other person who has their knife at your throat has malicious intent.

So far, scientists have found no way to eradicate prejudice completely, so all of the grant money that went into the research may have been for naught. There is just no proven way to make people completely unbiased, unless we replace the brain with a supercomputer. This brings about many more problems related to cybernetically-enhanced humans or artificial intelligence, but we're not going to discuss that here.

On the flip side, the good news is that while it is impossible to eliminate bias and prejudice, these two are not absolute states, meaning that one can have varying degrees of both, partly thanks to parental and peer conditioning and previous experience. The fact that you are reading this now means that you are probably a little less biased than your peers because you are aware of your own biases, which is a great starting point, and you are probably more curious and open to experience, which is also a great starting point.

So, what can we learn from all the research on biases? Here are four key recommendations:

Cognitive Diversity Must Be Embraced

All this means is that you must learn to accept that there are differences between people, even if you find yourself agreeing with someone who acts, thinks, feels, even speaks differently to you. One good way to begin is to watch a program on the television that you really don't like or listen to a radio show or podcast that you don't agree with. It won't be very comfortable to start with, but it will give you a few good ideas about the differences in people. From that starting point, you should begin to make an effort to get involved with people who don't like your values or who question them.

Empathy Must Be Cultivated

Empathy is one of the oldest topics in the study of psychology and it is defined as a willingness and/or ability to give due consideration to different points of view, to try to understand why other people feel and think the way they do. Plenty of training programs exist that are effective in boosting empathy, programs that have been successful even where the students are total psychopaths. Courses like that are not necessary for you; it is just as easy to practice empathy by yourself and learn to develop it.

Begin by trying to analyze what someone else may be thinking. See if you can understand their attitude or motive. To begin with, your results will be pretty random and way off, but what you are doing is training your mind to put itself in the place of another person. After that, you can try justifying why a person thinks and feels as they do.

Pay attention to the less privileged or disadvantaged; keep in mind that they may have come from a disadvantaged background and may not have had the luck or success that you have had. That doesn't mean that they are not talented, interesting, or that they don't work as hard as you do. Put yourself in their shoes; how would you feel? Think about what it must be like to be held back because you are different in some way.

Doing exercises like these are an easy way of helping you to get into empathic thinking, leading to more tolerance and less bias.

Your Biases Must Be Explicit

Determine your biases, and be honest with yourself. To deal with a bias, you must be certain that it exists and that you are aware of it. The best way is to take the Implicit Association test—it may not be perfect but it will give you a starting point from which you can identify hidden biases, those that you may not have known you had.

Once again, this won't stop you from being biased, but it does highlight the implicit and explicit biases. If you know that you are a racist or a sexist, and you are proud of being that way, this is not going to solve any problems for you. However, the very fact that you have made it this far through the book likely means that you are not racist or sexist and you have no pride in your biases.

Your Behaviors Must Be Controlled

What it all boils down to is that it doesn't matter what you think of or feel about others deep down. What really matters is your behavior—that is the biggest give-away to others whether you are biased or not; actions always speak louder than words and never more so than here. Nobody can be completely free of bias; what you must do is stop those biases from influencing the way you act.

Here's an example for you. Two people: one is thoroughly prejudiced but behaves, as best they can, in an inclusive and social manner, so much so, that everyone believes them to be a fair person. The second is very open-minded, has no real opinion on stereotypes but their behavior is that of a prejudiced person who speaks derogatorily about others.

You probably think this is a scenario that you are never likely to come across but, believe it or not, it is far more common than you will ever know. In simple terms, it is incredibly easy to be an advocate for something or someone if you don't have to show your actions to back it up. Look at the organ donation system—sure, there are millions of supporters, but how many have actually signed up to it? The environment—millions of people are advocates for saving the environment, but few of them follow that by living a lifestyle that is kind to the environment. Some people are prejudiced against socially disadvantaged groups but don't show it, while others are very open about their prejudices. That's life; it's the way we are.

When it comes down to it, we cannot live a life entirely free of bias, but we can learn to put ourselves in other people's shoes. When you can do that, you can question your biases and do something about stopping them from having an influence over how you think and act.

Part 3: Tools for the Mind

Cognitive Dissonance: The Power of Belief and How to Overcome It

In Part 3, we will go over actions, the things you can do to train your mind to be a better, less prejudiced thinker. We have a lot to cover here, but you do not need to do everything. You're infinitely better than most people, even if you only implement one of the methods that I will show you here.

Cognitive dissonance is simply the discomfort you experience on the inside that is caused when there is a conflict between your actions and behaviors, or beliefs and new information. For example, if you are a vegetarian and strictly do not eat meat, but you are forced to kill a rabbit and eat it because you are trying to avoid starvation in a life or death situation. Your longstanding belief compels you to stick to your vegetarian lifestyle, but the current situation forces you to either kill or perish. With that said, why do we experience cognitive dissonance?

We experience cognitive dissonance because our mind loves consistency. We all follow some sort of routine, which is a series of actions that occur at a certain time. For example, when you wake up in the morning, you will go to the toilet, brush your teeth, take a shower, get dressed, have breakfast, and go to work. This is a typical morning routine for many people, and we do this almost unconsciously. Our brain loves this sort of thing because it can streamline all actions to make them feel almost automatic. Even when you fold your arms, you always fold them a certain way, either the right tucked under the left or vice versa. If you try to do the opposite, you will feel strange.

We want consistency in our lives, and the lack thereof creates cognitive dissonance. Consistency here applies to our attitudes, habits, and view of the world at large. Whenever something happens that challenges that consistency, you will feel uncomfortable, and you will feel the urge to either reduce or eliminate the dissonance.

Psychologist Leon Festinger proposed a theory on cognitive dissonance. He suggested that we all strive toward internal consistency. It is not just a conscious goal, either. Achieving internal consistency is a psychological need. We all have the need to ensure that our beliefs and behavior align with each other. Inconsistency or conflicts between those two create an internal disharmony that we are programmed to avoid.

According to Festinger's 1957 book called *A Theory of Cognitive Dissonance*, he explained that one could understand cognitive dissonance as a condition that compels the subject to perform activities that reduce this dissonance. He compared it to how hunger compels us to eat to reduce hunger. Of course, cognitive dissonance is a much more powerful motivation, but it is basically that.

Influential Factors

Cognitive dissonance and the severity that people experience this dissonance will depend on some different factors, such as how highly they valued their said challenged belief and how inconsistent their belief is compared to their actions. Many factors may influence the overall strength of cognitive dissonance, including:

• If the challenged cognition is personal—such as belief in oneself—then the severity of the dissonance will be strong. The more personal it is, the stronger the dissonance becomes.

• The importance of cognition also plays a huge role. Other than personal beliefs, how much you value the cognition influences the strength of the dissonance when it occurs.

• The ratio that exists between consonant thoughts and dissonant thoughts. So, the more thoughts that are challenged, the stronger the dissonance is.

• The stronger the dissonance, the more a person feels the urge to remove uncomfortable feelings.

• Since cognitive dissonance compels us to take action to eliminate it, it can influence the way we act and behave in powerful ways.

Examples

Because cognitive dissonance happens when our beliefs and actions are conflicted, or our beliefs are challenged in some way, it can happen when we least expect it, and in any part of our lives. However, the effects are likely to be more significant when there is a strong conflict between behavior and those beliefs that we see as critical to self-identity.

For instance, cognitive dissonance can occur in the purchasing decisions that we make regularly. Take the electric car, for example. One would assume that switching to an electric car would be environmentally beneficial until they realize that the production of the electric car is just as bad for the environment.

In this case, we can see the conflict clearly. The person wants to contribute to the preservation of the environment by switching to an electric car but then finds out that the car may not be as environmentally friendly as they have been led to believe. However, in the long term, it will still cause less emissions into the atmosphere, but they feel guilt over the pollution from its production.

A dissonance occurs, and to reduce it, that person can either get rid of the car and take public transportation, or reduce their emphasis on environmental responsibility. So, as you can see, there are not many choices here when dissonance occurs between belief and action. Either remove the object that causes the dissonance or the belief.

Many of us are confident in our decision-making abilities, and there is also the tendency among humans to overestimate our abilities. In this case, if you made a bad purchase, then it will conflict with your self-belief, therefore causing cognitive dissonance.

Here, Festinger provided an example in his book on how a person might deal with cognitive dissonance when there is a conflict between behavior and health. You might have heard of this, but some people insist on smoking even though they know full well that smoking is unhealthy. In this case, the conflict is between the fact that smoking is bad and the contradicting behavior (smoking).

Therefore, smokers have two options to deal with the dissonance. They can quit smoking, or they can change their belief in the information they received. Some people go for the first option, which is the right one, whereas others opt to place a higher value on smoking than they do on their own health. The people in the second group do not reject the information. They acknowledge that smoking is unhealthy, but they believe that the chemical-induced pleasure they get from smoking is worth it.

There is a third option, and that is to decrease the drawbacks. In our example, the smoker may decide not to believe in the fact that smoking is unhealthy. They tell themselves that what they have heard about smoking so far is biased, so they may do their own research to find studies to prove that smoking is not unhealthy to counteract the new information that contradicts their belief. Alternatively, they may use superficial reasons to convince themselves to continue their behavior. In this case, they may tell themselves that they can't possibly avoid all potential risks out there, so there's no point in avoiding this one.

The smokers may also try to convince themselves that they will gain weight if they stop smoking, which is often true based on numerous studies. The thing is that stopping smoking will only cause you to gain a couple of pounds. There are cases in which people gain much more than that, but the chance is very rare. What the smoker sees is not the insignificant consequence of gaining a few kilos, but rather the fact that they gain weight, and that is a health risk associated with weight gain. So, smokers convince themselves that smoking is not at all bad considering that quitting smoking would cause weight gain.

Common Reaction to Cognitive Dissonance

People feel compelled to reduce cognitive dissonance depending on the severity. There are three common responses that they will display:

• **Shift Focus:** here, the person simply focusses on the supportive beliefs, thus outweighing the discomfort caused by the dissonance. For example, those who feel strongly about the environment may experience extreme cognitive dissonance when they drive a car that burns lots of fuel very quickly. In this case, they may choose to do their own research to find out whether they are contributing to the detriment of the environment. They find out the facts that verify their actions, therefore reducing the discomfort.

• **Reduce Importance:** in the second scenario, let's say that Steve leads a healthy lifestyle, but he works at the office that requires him to sit for eight hours a day, which is unhealthy. The dissonance then occurs when he realizes that sitting for too long is associated with various health problems. He might not be able to request a standing desk, nor can he work by sitting and standing up intermittently. So, his only option is to find ways to justify his behavior, which he can do in many ways, since he can cover up the dissonant action with other activities that support the conflicting belief. Steve may decide to stick to his healthy lifestyle or continue to incorporate more healthy habits to compensate for the conflict.

• **Change the Belief:** finally, you can also choose to change the conflicting belief, so that it aligns with your behavior. This is considered to be the best way to deal with cognitive dissonance if the conflicting belief is a limiting belief. However, changing one's belief is difficult, especially if that belief has to do with deeply ingrained values such as religion.

How Does It Feel to Have Cognitive Dissonance?

Every person has their own levels of tolerance for cognitive dissonance, and, for that reason, it cannot be objectively measured. Some will only experience a mild level of discomfort, a gut feeling that something is wrong, but not severe enough to bring about a sense of urgency or cause any major problems for them. Some will want to make changes to remove that discomfort straight away, and that's no bad thing.

However, the worst-case is a powerful dissonance that causes anxiety, more so when it is affecting a deep value or belief, like morality or religion. For example, growing up in a strict religion that teaches you that having sex before you get married is sinful; if you then get involved in a sexual relationship before you are married, you are likely to feel a strong cognitive dissonance.

To a certain extent, one community affected by cognitive dissonance is the LGBT+ community, although things are not as bad as they used to be. If, for example, you were taught that it was wrong to have sexual feelings about a person of the same sex, you may begin to experience strong feelings of embarrassment, guilt, anger, or shame if you do, and that comes from cognitive dissonance. If it is strong enough, you might even begin to believe that you are immoral, a degenerate even, and you could start to hate yourself until you can resolve the dissonance.

Three Ways to Decrease Cognitive Dissonance

Cognitive dissonance is peppered throughout our lives; some of it is tolerable while some of it is powerful—the latter makes us want to make immediate changes. It is almost impossible to achieve consistency throughout our lives because all that we do and believe will be challenged at some point, requiring changes to be made. According to experts, there are three ways that we can all decrease cognitive dissonance:

- **Change How You Behave:** cognitive dissonance rears its head when your actions and beliefs are in conflict. One way of decreasing dissonance is to change the belief or action that caused it. For example, if you drink and drive regularly, the way to decrease dissonance is to stop—stop drinking altogether or stop driving when you drink—and teach yourself that it is not okay to drive when under the influence. By doing this, actions and beliefs are harmonized, and dissonance is eliminated or at least significantly decreased.

- **Change Your Beliefs:** the human brain creates a lens, and it is through this that our reality is perceived. Your reality may be different from those around you, and reality perception is constantly being altered to relieve dissonant feelings. What that means is that the human mind will filter out anything that doesn't fit with its beliefs, so dissonance is only experienced when it is completely unavoidable. For example, smokers may constantly look for information about the link between smoking and cancer, choosing to believe the research that says there is no real link. This is biased behavior, but smokers continue to do this as a way of reducing dissonance and carrying on as before.

- **Justifying Your Behavior and Beliefs:** this is never a good idea when those beliefs and behaviors can potentially harm others, and when "bad" behavior is in conflict with a "good" belief. Let's take the person who just loves to spend money; they may be continually convincing themselves that they can't take the money with them when they die, so they may as well spend it, or, simply, that money is earned to be spent. Another example would be the person who gets involved in something risky; they may justify this by saying that life is there for the living, and that you just don't know when your time is up. We could flip things around, say that the action is "good," and the belief is "bad"—there would still be cognitive dissonance, but you would be opening up the potential to change the bad belief.

Cognitive Dissonance and Emotionally Draining Relationships

We have all been involved with or know someone who is with a person who drains energy, known as an "energy vampire." These people use abusive tactics, like physical and emotional abuse, intimidating behavior, sexual abuse, social isolation, economic abuse, and many more damaging behaviors, just to keep control over the victim. The threat of abuse is always hanging over the victim, and, as time goes on, it gets worse.

Victims tend to ignore gut feelings, not believing in them when it comes to these kinds of relationships. Deep down, they know it's all wrong; they know that they are the victim in an abusive relationship, but they continue to stay, living in fear of what could happen, in the mistaken hope that things will get better.

This causes a deep cognitive dissonance because the victim wants to believe that everything will be okay, while knowing that it won't. They want to believe that if they show their partner love and attention, he or she will change. The reality is very different, because "energy vampires" have no idea what love is. Their idea of love is to continue the abuse; shaming, criticizing, and punishing their partner.

The main defense mechanism of anyone caught in such a relationship is to do whatever they can to decrease the dissonance. There are those three ways we talked about earlier, but these are the least resistive methods and will do nothing to ease things for the victim. Nothing is going to change, and they won't feel any safer.

A victim of this type of relationship may, for example, lie: convincing themselves that their partner really does love them, as a way of justifying what is happening. They tell themselves that when a good thing happens, everything will change for the better, but every time they are subjected to more abuse, the dissonance just becomes stronger.

There is a good reason why a victim should get out as quickly as possible—changes in the brain. The longer you live with cognitive dissonance, the more likely it is your brain will change, similar to how it does with PTSD. Physical symptoms may manifest themselves as autoimmune diseases, and victims may even experience certain brain disorders. Once that happens, the victim is no longer able to think properly, they cannot see a way out, and things will not change until they learn to have trust in themselves once more. There are ways that this kind of situation can be fixed, though, using therapies such as

Tapping or Eye Movement Desensitization and Reprocessing (EMDR) therapy.

How to Decrease Dissonance Following a Relationship with an Energy Vampire

If you have been caught in a relationship with an energy vampire, it will take more than just reduction techniques to build you back up. Obviously, the first step is to remove yourself from the relationship. Then you can begin the process of recovery.

Aside from the methods mentioned above, there is one more way to deal with cognitive dissonance after this kind of relationship. The victim must get some validation for the situation—therapy with a professional, chatting to a friend, writing it all down, and so on.

Neuroplasticity: Change Your Limiting Beliefs Now

As the name suggests, neuroplasticity is a term used to describe the flexibility of the mind. More accurately, it is the ability of the mind to be molded, like plastic, based on thoughts and behavior. Indeed, it does not matter how old you are; your mind can still be changed for the better. But before we dive too deeply into this, let's start from the beginning.

How Beliefs Are Formed and How to Change Them

Everyone is different. That fact has already been established. No two bodies are identical, and no two individuals have exactly the same life experiences, thinking patterns, and personalities. The way our bodies function is also not exactly identical either. In the diet and lifestyle world, it has been proven that two people will get different results from the same diet even if they follow it to the letter. This difference is also present in our psyche. We each have a belief set that shapes our individual lives.

I've probably mentioned and will mention this several times, but it is worth stressing the fact that we perceive the world through a lens constructed by our beliefs. This influences how we see ourselves and everything around us. Therefore, our beliefs have a powerful influence on our actions and emotions. As a result, our success and happiness also depend on our beliefs. This is exactly why successful people always tell us to believe in ourselves if we want to be successful. There is no precise recipe for success other than self-belief.

What is a Belief?

So, with that said and done, what exactly is a "belief?" Simply put, a belief is something that we think is true. Pay attention here because the keyword here is "think." Just because we think something is true does not make it true.

Therefore, belief is anything we assume is true, and we use it to help us understand the world, to navigate it. Think of it as a system to help us operate in this world. It can even save our lives, because a belief can influence what we do and feel. Since belief is a safety mechanism, we are naturally inclined to protect and preserve our beliefs once this system is formed.

Our beliefs work at the subconscious level, much like the autopilot system in a self-driving car, for example. When you form a belief and give it enough time to become reinforced, you start to take it for granted and never question whether your beliefs are accurate or not.

We all have different sets of beliefs, meaning that we all have different perceptions of reality. Two people can disagree quite passionately about a particular subject, leading to conflict, all because of a difference in beliefs. Some good examples include politics, traditionalism and modernism, death sentences, abortion, et cetera.

On a more personal level, our beliefs also change how we see challenges or any problems. Some see them as a setback and another reason to give up, whereas others see them as a learning opportunity and a stepping-stone to success.

How Are Beliefs Formed?

Have you ever wondered why children need to go to school and receive education early on when they could probably do better when they are adults? To help you understand why, think of our minds in this way: when we arrive in this world, our minds are like blank canvases or a wet piece of clay. We start with a clean slate that has limitless possibilities. That means that when we were kids, we had no preconceived beliefs. What we had were curiosity and the powers of observation.

Since children know so little about the world, the only way they can learn is from others around them. That means learning from their parents, teachers, friends, and other people they encounter. So, your core beliefs are pretty much formed by external factors that are well outside of your control.

From this, we can identify two main sources of beliefs. The first is the acceptance of what others tell us to be facts, which is often what children do. But as we grow older, another factor comes into play that arguably has a more powerful influence on our beliefs, and that is our past experiences.

Here's an example of how beliefs are formed. Suppose that during one Thanksgiving dinner, you (as a kid) didn't eat all of your dinner because you already felt full. It could be because the serving size was too big or you had too many cookies before the meal, but the cause didn't matter—what mattered then was the fact that your parents saw that you still had some food left, and they reprimanded you for it. They may have told you that good children eat everything on their plates or they pointed out the fact that the world is full of starving children, and you not finishing the food meant that you were ungrateful. Although the actual message that your parents may have wanted to tell you was that one should never be wasteful, the way that they phrased this lesson influenced your beliefs in more ways than one.

At that point, if we take what our parents said to heart and believe that it is true, then they have planted a seed of belief that will manifest itself. In this case, that means you will grow up believing that good children should eat every last bit of food that they are served, no matter how much or little there is. This could either lead to malnutrition or overeating, more so in the latter case if you have a grandmother, for example, who is very generous with her portion sizes. Another belief formed here is that we think disagreeing with our parents would mean that we were being "ungrateful," which is a really powerful label for children. All of these beliefs would have been further reinforced whenever we did not finish our food and got reprimanded for it.

Having something as personal as our core beliefs being shaped by outside factors may seem like a bad idea but, to be fair, we need to learn from others around us. Just like every other aspect of our lives, we have to start somewhere. It does not matter so much about what beliefs we've formed so far, because we could not stop them from being formed in the past. What matters is what we can do right now about it. What is learned can be unlearned, and the same applies here. You can change your beliefs.

But our minds still undergo further changes when we leave home and attend schools and meet more people. For one, the teachers will also tell you what they think is true and right. Again, since we have no prior experience in life, at least other than what our parents—or parental figures—have already told us, we also accept what our teachers tell us to be true.

For example, suppose that you didn't do very well in math (partly because the teacher did not do a good job teaching it), your teacher may tell you that you are bad at math or you are lazy. Then, you start to believe what the teacher has told you, especially when they do it several times. Eventually, you come to believe that you are actually bad at math, or you truly believe that you are lazy, even though that is false.

When you are at school, you are subject to more influence from your peers and classmates, because you spend more time with them than your teachers. Suppose they decide to bully you by calling you nasty names or even going as far as being physically abusive; you may feel that whatever they call you is true, and you will feel defenseless.

So, the moment that we accept that something is a fact, a belief is formed, and it is ingrained into the subconscious mind. When that happens, it will be difficult to remove that belief because it is not something that you can just consciously reach into. While you can reason with your conscious mind to discern truth from falsehood, the subconscious mind cannot be reasoned with. It takes our beliefs and uses them as a reference to form our perception of the world and automate our responses.

How Our Beliefs Affect Our Behavior, Emotions, and Thoughts

Here's an example that we can all relate to. I'm certain that you have crossed roads multiple times in your life. Take a moment now and think of how you act when you need to get across a busy road. For one, you may notice that you follow a set of behaviors automatically. You first look each way to ensure the road is clear for you to walk across. Sometimes, you might even run across just to get to the other side quicker. If you see a car coming your way when you are crossing the street, you may feel tense. Just crossing the street alone, regardless of the traffic, can be anxiety-inducing for many people. Whatever and however you do it, the chances are that you do it consistently. You have the brain to thank for automating the entire process.

What I want to point out is not how one should cross the road, but rather how the automated system in our brain is created. You see, the way you cross the street is the product of only one of countless other beliefs. All of these combined create a complex system of automatic responses and thoughts. Some of the beliefs are true and useful, and others are harmful, as they are not based on facts.

When a belief is recently developed, it is easy to change it because it hasn't spent enough time in our minds. However, when a belief has been reinforced over and over, across several years, it becomes so deeply rooted that we simply fail to perceive the reality that contradicts that belief. Our mind simply throws away all reason and only looks for the information that validates and reinforces our belief to avoid cognitive dissonance. Why does the mind do that?

You see, humans are lazy creatures. We want things to be as easy as possible, and our mind is like that as well. It always goes on the path of least resistance. In this case, one can either change the longstanding-belief or change how information is perceived. The easiest thing to do would be to change how one interprets information.

That means it does not really matter how the information is presented. No matter how convincing it looks, if it is a direct contradiction to your longstanding belief in the subconscious mind, you won't acknowledge a single word. Plus, since our beliefs change how we see the world, and our thoughts, actions, and emotions are our response to the world, that means that our beliefs also influence them.

For example, let's say that you believe that dogs are dangerous. Maybe your parents told you that, or you have been horribly maimed in the past by the neighbor's pit bull. As a result, you have a powerful belief in the dangers of these lovely mutts and would do everything in your power to avoid contact with them. This impulse causes your mind to develop various automatic responses to anything related to dogs.

You might feel anxious, and your body tenses up when you even sense the presence of a dog because you see it as an impending danger. If you see one growling and adopting an aggressive stance, then you'll see it as a threat. You may recall the time when you got bitten or remember your parent's warning, and you will feel threatened.

Because you develop the belief that dogs are aggressive and dangerous creatures, you won't even notice a friendly dog. You will still see that pup as a threat, and you will respond accordingly. It's almost as if we see the world through a lens with filters created by the beliefs ingrained in our subconscious minds.

As I've mentioned before, beliefs may be both beneficial and limiting. When you start to question your own beliefs, you will see which is which. Negative or limiting beliefs stop us from reaching our full potential. However, positive or empowering beliefs are based on facts and logic. They let us remain resilient and thrive in the face of hardship.

In a way, our beliefs shape our view of reality. The thing is that not many people notice that because our beliefs are so obscure that we do not take time out to scrutinize our sense of reality. Since our beliefs change our view of reality, thoughts, and behaviors, they also influence how successful we can be in life. One person may see a problem as a challenge to overcome, whereas another may see it as a dead-end, all because of their beliefs. You don't even need to look far to find such examples. You might even know some of those people personally, those who managed to overcome all odds and those who gave up at the slightest hint of inconvenience, even though they had all the resources and ability they needed to overcome the problem.

These are just a few of the ways that one situation is viewed differently by different people. Bear in mind that we all try to do whatever we can to reinforce our beliefs, to validate them, because it is so much easier to wrongly interpret something than it is to change what we believe in. Everyone feels, thinks, and acts in a way that they see as appropriate. We could even go so far as to say that strong beliefs will create self-fulfillment.

Now we understand the importance of beliefs; we need to look a little closer at them. It's great when you have all "good" beliefs, but if you can identify your beliefs and eliminate the limiting ones from your subconscious, you will go a long way. It isn't going to be easy, but then nothing worth having is. After all, nobody wants to live their life confined by beliefs that only make them unhappy, which stops them from achieving their potential.

Identifying Negative or Limiting Beliefs

The first step to change is not to out-right challenge your limiting beliefs. You want to first discern the good from the bad. This will take some time because you will have many beliefs to analyze. I recommend spending some time alone at home on the weekend and asking yourself a bunch of questions to identify limiting beliefs. It will take a long time and require a lot of effort. It won't be comfortable for you either, if you do it right.

Nonetheless, I want to point out again that finding limiting beliefs and replacing them with empowering ones will be worth the trouble. You will know this the moment you manage to uproot a limiting belief and replace it with an empowering belief. It is a life-changing experience.

So, try to find some time alone in a place you won't be disturbed. Have a pen and a notebook ready. Then, ask yourself a lot of questions. Here are a few to get you started:
- "What are the things that I want, but fail to get?"
- "What do I want to improve, but I never get the result I want?"
- "What areas of my life do I feel incompetent about?"

These are only a few questions that you can ask yourself. It will be a soul-searching journey, so you want to take your time with this one. The idea is that you identify what areas in life you are falling behind with, how and why that happened, and you might find the limiting belief behind it all. These questions may look simply, but these will be some of the most difficult ones you will ever ask yourself, as they should be. You won't get the real answer immediately, and it will take a lot of time and brutal honesty. The latter is definitely going to be difficult for you, as it requires you to accept the reality of your beliefs, and this may cause cognitive dissonance. Since we're talking about deeply rooted beliefs, the dissonance will be strong. No matter how strong it is, you might want to develop another belief by telling yourself that if you make the change and endure the pain, it will be worth your efforts.

Replacing Limiting Beliefs

Once all your limiting beliefs have been identified, you can begin to eliminate them and replace them with empowering beliefs. It isn't enough just to eliminate the limiting ones from your life; you need to develop the most empowering beliefs that you can. None of this will be easy; your brain and mind are no longer a clean slate, and changing everything you thought you believed in will be hard.

Since our brain loves consistency, we can use that to our advantage. To change your beliefs, you will need consistency and time, lots of it.

The task itself is simple. Anyone can do that, but your success relies on whether you can stick to it. Take it as slowly as you need to—as long as you can stick to it consistently. Consistency is what is important here. There is no need to rush something as delicate as this.

Just like anything man-made, we can unlearn limiting beliefs and form empowering ones. So, here are the things you need to do:

1. Choose one limiting belief; think hard about how it has worked against you previously. In doing so, you are establishing the fact that you have good reasons to want to remove it. The best way to do this is by isolating it by contrasting it with all the empowering beliefs you have. It will create a dissonance, but your mind will be convinced that the best way to eliminate the dissonance is by removing the limiting belief. For example, suppose that you have trust issues. You are convinced that everyone is out there trying to exploit you. Ask yourself why you have this belief. Maybe you had a terrible break-up because your spouse cheated on you. Maybe you never really have any friends. Perhaps you simply believe that trusting someone is a sign of weakness since you can get hurt when they are not honest with you. Then, look at how this belief has harmed you. Maybe no one at work really likes you. You live mostly in isolation, and you feel lonely. Perhaps you even feel guilty for pushing away the people that genuinely care about you.

2. Look for the evidence proving that a belief is not true; when you can accept that the belief is harming your life, you can then reinforce this fact, and that a particular limiting belief is not good for you. To do this, you need to find more evidence to convince yourself. Going back to the distrust example we used before, you might think back to when a person you were dating was very honest with you about something, something that caused discomfort and damaged your relationship. Perhaps you can think of times when you were at school, and a group of kids you didn't know allowed you to sit with them at lunch. And, no doubt, you can think of a time when you took a chance on trusting a person and it worked out for you, perhaps of a good friend you had in the past who never lied to you and didn't, at any time, ever fail you. Basically, find evidence from your past experience and acknowledge that all of those events happened. Allow them to sink in to the point where you accept and have been convinced that the limiting belief is not true. I recommend spending as much time as you need on the first two steps here because you can still receive many benefits by just removing limiting beliefs alone. You don't have to focus on incorporating empowering beliefs if you do not want to. One less negative and limiting belief is an amazing improvement already.

3. **The next step is to start planting the seed of an empowering belief;** going back to the last example, try telling yourself that it's only a small minority of people that are dishonest, and you know that from your own experiences. By now, you have sufficient evidence for this belief to be established, and by doing so, you can release the limiting belief, admit that it wasn't true, acknowledge the fact that it has just been getting in your way all this time, and move on—begin believing that most people are naturally honest.

4. **Finally, it's a matter of reinforcing the empowering belief;** to do this, you must constantly remind yourself of the new empowering belief. This is not going to be easy, given how long you have had the old limiting beliefs. Do not go into this with the expectation that the empowering belief will just magically embed itself in your subconscious straight away. It's going to take time, and it's going to take consistency, especially where limiting beliefs have long been ingrained in you. The recommendation is this—whenever you can, remind yourself that you have a new belief; the more you do it, the more that new belief will become embedded and reinforced. And the more reinforced it is, the more empowering it will be. Try to remind yourself every morning and every night if you can.

Our belief systems are very powerful because they influence every aspect of our lives, including how we think, feel, and act. Unfortunately, something this important is so obscure that many people fail to see it. People take their beliefs for granted and believe that whatever it is they believe in to be facts, which is often not the case. When we take the time and effort to examine our own beliefs closely, we can then start to root out the limiting beliefs that stop us from living the best life we can live. From there, we can start to replace those limiting thoughts with the ones that will empower us in ways that we could never imagine.

Taking Advantage of Neuroplasticity

Take a moment now and observe—how do you converse with yourself? How would you describe your life to others? Do you fault-find in just about every aspect of your life? Now think about the language you use when you talk to others, or talk about them—is it the same as you do about you and your own life?

We go through our days without conscious observation of our thoughts. The world is busy; we are busy; we are simply too bogged down with other things that we just don't have time to listen to our own minds. When we do stop and take time to listen, we are surprised, perhaps even shocked at how much negativity we use when we talk to ourselves. That negativity may overwhelm you and leave you feeling like you have no power over your mind; no power over the direction your mind wants to take you in.

We have always had the belief that our brains were hard-wired, and there was no way of changing them. Wasn't everyone born with an inherited trait that made them special and gifted in some way? Now we know that is not true and that our brains are constantly changing.

Just one thought has the potential to determine how our brain is structured. The more compassionate you are when you talk with yourself, the easier you find it to pick yourself up and carry on when you fail at something.

We've all heard Gandhi's quote: "Your beliefs become your thoughts, your thoughts become your words, your words become your actions, your actions become your habits, your habits become your values, and your values become your destiny."

Neuroplasticity is an emerging scientific field. Put simply, neuroplasticity is how the brain can mold itself into different shapes, much like plastic can be molded. It is how the brain forms neural connections so it can reorganize itself. In this way, we know that the brain can be changed and, although it takes time, we know that we can teach it new tricks.

Over time, our understanding of neuroplasticity has changed, bringing about a new treatment for dyslexia, cancer prevention, injury, and stroke victims. But it doesn't just work in medical and scientific fields; we can also apply what we know about it to every part of our lives, and the process of that is simple.

The changes happen in all parts of our brains, including the amygdala and the cingulate cortex but, for those of you that are not neuroscientists, you don't really need to understand how the brain is affected by those changes. Medical and scientific names are irrelevant; all that matters is how simple it all is.

So far, we've only touched on the basics of the human brain; it is an incredibly complex machine, and the details about how the changes happen are also complex. The most important thing is that you can change your brain by using your mind.

Bear in mind that all these changes mean the human brain is rewiring itself all the time. Sometimes those wires will be all over the place; other times, it will reinforce the positive and not the negative thoughts. Evolution has meant that our brains have developed a bad habit—we cling to negativity, mostly for survival, rather than discarding it. Rewiring your brain requires you to do it all yourself by controlling your own mind.

When you were younger, somebody did all of your thinking for you, leaving you with no choice. Now that you are an adult you have to make your own choices. All that negative self-talk has already done a number on your brain, and it's guided you down your life path so far—now you need to stop it, rebuild that path in another, more positive direction.

Ground-breaking research, a combination of Eastern practices and Western science, was carried out by Harvard Medical School and the University of Wisconsin. The research was done to see what power the mind has over shaping the brain.

Professor Richard Davidson wanted to look at how meditation affected the brain; the fourteenth Dalai Lama provided him with twelve Tibetan Buddhists with a combined amount of over 10,000 meditation hours between them. In Buddhism, it is believed that compassion and meditation can only change someone for the better, but those are just two of many Buddhist practices. This research was the first time that we had been able to study how meditation affected us; all we knew was that it changed something, but we didn't know what. The results of the study suggested that meditation can change the way the brain is structured, but not only that, it can change how it functions too. It was seen that the subjects had gamma wave activity in their brains that was more powerful than anything ever seen before.

Gamma brain activity governs our cognitive functioning, learning, memory, consciousness, perception, etc., meaning that changes are best introduced once the gamma brain activity increases. It takes practice to increase activity in that area, but you don't have to become a monk to do so. Simple mindfulness practices such as meditation are powerful enough to change the way the brain is structured, particularly in the areas connected with compassion and awareness.

With that said, you can induce positive changes in your brain by undoing the faulty configurations that have plagued you for so long. Consider doing the following:

Awareness

As with anything in life, to make a change, you must recognize your current situation and the need to make that change. In this case, to make positive changes in the brain, one must recognize the problems in there first. So, learn to recognize negative thoughts. This is fairly simple.

Start by listening to the way you talk to yourself and ask yourself how you would feel if someone else were to tell you the same thing. If you think that it is unacceptable for someone to tell you the things you tell yourself, then the chances are that you are too hard on yourself.

Other than that, I recommend you write down the negative thoughts on a notepad and go over it once a week. Do this for a month, and you should have a fairly extensive list of negative self-talk. When you look at the list, try to see if you can identify certain patterns that may lead to a bigger underlying problem. Maybe you'll see that your negative self-talk comes from your deteriorating relationship, lack of career advancement, et cetera.

Whatever you do, never judge your own negative thoughts. Just recognize that you have negative thoughts. Why? Because you want to learn to cut yourself some slack as well. When you judge your negative self-talk, you are partially judging and blaming yourself, and that is not the path to self-compassion. Acknowledge that you have been talking to yourself in a bad way, but forgive yourself and focus your energy on improving yourself instead.

When you are going about your daily life, watch the way that you converse with yourself. If you start thinking negatively, stop; breathe deeply, tell yourself that you will extend the same compassion to yourself that you do to others. In short, be a compassionate observer of your own mind without judgment.

Find the Silver Lining

Simply put, find something good out of the bad situation you find yourself in. We have a bad habit when it comes to how we see problems. We all have them; maybe it's the bad economy and massive layoffs; a difficult boss; or that your company's culture is toxic. Maybe it's your mean and unsupportive family; or you don't have enough resources, education, experience, or finances to get what you want. The list goes on and on.

Many people don't know that what is really holding them back isn't the problem itself. It's how they see their problems and the story they tell themselves about them. The things that you tell yourself may just be excuses to keep you inside your comfort zone. So, be honest with yourself and see problems as they are, but not worse than they are. Life is full of problems, but instead of seeing them as obstacles, see them as stepping stones.

Morning Routine

First, let us start with the morning routine. What is yours like? Does it consist of you waking up to the blaring alarm, feeling groggy, and cursing yourself for staying up late so you could watch "Just one more" episode of the latest and hottest Netflix series? Is it all about coffee and email and everyone else's needs first? If so, then you need to freshen up your morning. You want to have a morning with intention and direction instead of the chaos and distractions we all are too familiar with.

You need to have a consistent morning routine, so you are free from distractions, feel energetic, are present in the moment and enjoy life—while maintaining that beautiful creative flow and making good life decisions.

Again, you want to start small. You don't have to overhaul your morning routine completely. So, do the following small things in the morning:

1. No more excuses. We all say that we're not a morning person and so it's natural that your morning is always a mess. I'll tell you this now: no one is born a morning person. It takes a conscious effort to establish a morning routine and remain consistent with it. So, start your morning routine whenever your morning starts.

2. Gratitude stretch. I understand that this sounds like a bit of a "stretch"—pardon the pun. But when you wake up, you want to stretch your muscles to let them know that it is time to get busy again. Don't forget to stretch your abs because the arms and legs aren't enough. While you are at it, try to come up with three things you are grateful for and say them to yourself.

3. Ignore the notifications. Just ignore those for now to create a little haven from the digital world for the first waking hour. You want your morning to be stress-free and without distractions. So that means not going online or checking your phone for any messages if you can help it. You don't want to get distracted with Facebook updates or become stressed when you check the emails from your boss. You want to start the day on your own terms. If you really need to catch up and get ready for the day ahead, do it at the last moment, so you know what to expect before you go to work. This brings us to the fourth step.

4. Go outside. Get out there, really. You want to start your day with fresh air in your lungs and sunshine on your face. If possible, I recommend you do more than just standing outside on your porch or balcony to enjoy the view. That is fine, but if you can get out and have a short walk around the neighborhood, that is even better.

5. Go inside. After you have soaked in the beauty and energy of the morning, head inside and do something more for your mind. I'm talking about reflection, meditation, praying, or simply just sit and be in the present moment. Spend a few minutes here and pay attention to how you are feeling. We all have asked other people how they are, but so few of us have stopped and asked ourselves how we are. Your body and heart will tell you, and this can lead to more questions and answers. Taking the time to ask yourself these questions can be relieving in itself. Just pay attention to your body and mind.

6. Create a morning "not-to-do" list. This is a reverse concept of a to-do list. You might have a better idea of what you want to do in the morning by making it clear what you *don't* want to do. These are the things that don't add value to your morning, so spend some time figuring out what they are. Things such as social media and YouTube are definitely on the list.

7. Show up. Even if you cannot follow through with all of these recommendations, I suggest that you at least do something during your morning routine. That may be doing yoga for only five minutes or stretching in your bedroom, whatever you would like to do. Try to stick to a routine for at least a week. Start sorting out your morning plan and stick to it, but do it at your own pace.

Meditation

Meditation should be part of your morning or evening routine. It serves as a tool to calm your mind. Think of meditation as a transitional period, from a relaxed to an alert state at the start of the day, and vice versa at the end of the day. Meditation allows your body and mind to unwind and prepare for sleep. In the end, you will have a clearer mind, a more restful sleep, and other benefits. In this case, it can also be a tool to fight sugar cravings.

Meditation has many forms, but the most popular one is guided meditation because it is beginner-friendly. If you can, I recommend the traditional meditation in which no tools are needed. All you need is a quiet and open space free from distraction. A meditation bench or mat is unnecessary unless you have back pain. Other props are completely unnecessary.

Once you have found that perfect meditation space, simply sit down on the floor in a meditation pose or sit on a chair with your back straight, make sure that your back is not leaning against the wall or the backrest. The idea here is to get you to practice mindfulness and concentration at the same time.

Once you get in your position, simply close your eyes and start breathing from your diaphragm. This is the best way of breathing as you can fully fill your lungs with air as you breathe in. Your stomach should rise as you breathe in. If your shoulders or chest move, then you are breathing from the chest, which is shallow breathing and is an incorrect way to breathe.

As you breathe, focus on your own breathing, which practices concentration. At the same time, make sure you are aware of your own thoughts and posture, which is a mindfulness practice. If your mind starts to wander, gently guide your mind back to your own breathing. If you start to slouch, straighten your back.

If you use guided meditation, you will be given instructions throughout the meditation process. If you follow the traditional meditation practice, you will need a timer. Your phone will do, so long as you set it to "Do Not Disturb" mode so no one can reach you while you meditate.

If you are new to meditation, I recommend you spend only two minutes for the first one or two weeks. You can then increase it to five, then ten minutes once you are comfortable.

Personally, I have a clock that makes a ticking sound every second. So, I focus on the ticking sound and count it each time. Five seconds to inhale, one-second hold, five seconds exhale, and one-second hold. That means I spend twelve seconds for the whole breathing cycle. If I repeat this cycle ten times, then I get 120 seconds of meditation, which is two minutes.

By following this meditation style, you can do the math and find out exactly how many breathing cycles you need to do based on the time you want to spend in meditation. Five minutes of meditation equals twenty-five breathing cycles. Ten minutes of meditation equals fifty breathing cycles.

At first, it will be difficult, especially for those who lead busy lives and need to think all the time. Meditation should be the last thing you do before you hit the hay and one of the first things you do in the morning. This is what you should be doing to have a calm morning and a restful sleep, but you should do more in order to fight sugar cravings. You can use it to break the behavioral pattern that leads you straight to needing sugar.

Whenever a sugar craving strikes, drop whatever you're doing immediately and do a quick meditation. If you're at home, you should have a meditation spot already. If you're outside or at work, you can just meditate while sitting in your chair. Just put your hands on your knees, close your eyes, and breathe deeply. How long you plan to stay that way depends on the situation, but try to go for five minutes if you can. That's twenty-five breathing cycles. In the end, you should feel the craving subside.

How to Solve Any Problem

What do you do when you have a problem to solve? Do you charge straight at it, or do you sweep it under the rug and hope it goes away? Either of these options is not the best way to solve your problems. Although one should be commended for not shying away from problems and choosing to dive headfirst into the problem, if you do so without prior planning, then you stand a good chance of failing spectacularly.

Some problems do go away if you leave them there for a while, but those problems are most likely the things that you should not concern yourself with anyway. But the problems that persist will cause a lot of harm to your life if you don't address them as soon as possible.

So, what you need is an effective approach to problem-solving that covers all your bases so you can remain organized and on top of your game. What you need is a system to help you think systematically. Here is a 10-step system to enhance your critical thinking and problem-solving skills:

1. Rephrase

First of all, you need to change how you view the problem. To be more precise, you need to use a more positive description of your situation. In fact, the word "problem" carries a negative label. It suggests that something is wrong.

So, instead of calling it a problem, call it a challenge or an opportunity to learn. A positive description of the situation also influences how you view and approach it. Calling it a challenge may even encourage you to come up with creative solutions.

2. Define the Situation Clearly

The last thing you want to do is to put yourself in a situation where you have no clue what is going on and what is at stake. So, ask yourself what exactly is going on and identify the sources of your stress, anxiety, and worry, as well as why they make you feel that way. Make sure to write down your answers and be as precise as possible.

3. Use Critical Thinking

The next step would be to analyze the problem and explore your options. Before you jump straight into it, ask yourself what else is the problem because you may overlook the bigger issue at hand. To verify whether there is something else you need to address, keep asking yourself the same question until you no longer get superficial answers.

Maybe the issue you are experiencing is only the symptom and not the disease, so to speak. The same thing applies to problem-solving. You want to get to the root of the problem.

When you have identified the root cause, take some time to think about how you could approach it. The keyword here is "could," not "should." For now, just brainstorm different solutions because there is almost always more than one solution to a problem. Find out what you can do about it and write down your possible course of action.

4. Define the Ideal Solution

Next, you want to identify your criteria for success, so you know what the best course of action is. The ideal solution should address most, if not all, the criteria for success. To help you figure out what they are, ask yourself the following questions:

- "What are the things that must be addressed?"
- "What problems should the solution address?"
- "What would the ideal outcome be?"

In short, you want to know what conditions you need to meet to consider the problem "solved." You may end up with a long list of conditions, so you want to prioritize which condition you want to address first.

Of course, when you identify the conditions for success, you also define failure, and that is the failure to meet the conditions. This is why most people do not define their success. But this step is necessary because if you want to solve problems properly, you need to know exactly what success looks like to you.

5. Pick the Best Solution

When you define the conditions for success, you should have a clear idea of what solution is best for the problem. The best solution should be the one that checks as many boxes as possible, or all the boxes that matter.

6. Prepare for the Worst

Keep in mind that literally, everything can go wrong, even when you plan meticulously. There are only a finite number of factors that you can control, and you pretty much have to rely on luck in certain areas. So, when you plan a course of action, remember that things can go wrong. Study how things can go wrong. You don't have to analyze all the possible unfavorable outcomes. You just need to be aware of the worst thing that could happen.

Proper planning accounts for what *can* happen, not what *should* happen. So, you want to have a contingency plan ready just in case things go wrong. You may need to make some compromises, but if you cannot accept that, try the next best solution.

7. Measure Your Progress

Next, set up measures based on your decision. This is different from defining success criteria. It's about setting up markers to measure your progress. So, ask yourself the following questions:
- "How will I measure success?"
- "How will I compare the success of this solution against that of another?"

Of course, defining the criteria means that you need something to measure your progress. Think of something that can be easily tracked that relates to your success.

8. Take Complete Responsibility

Take full responsibility for the implementation of the decision. Did you know that many people in this world have had the most creative ideas, but they never materialized? It is because the owner of the ideas is specifically assigned the responsibility for carrying out the decision. When you have a responsibility, you take action; without it, you will not. So, take complete responsibility.

9. Set a Deadline

To claim full responsibility for your solution, you also need to set a deadline to add that bit of pressure to get things done. A decision without a deadline is worthless. If it is a major decision that will take a long time to implement, consider setting a series of short-term deadlines and a schedule for reporting.

Remember what we just discussed about measuring your progress? You can use those as sub-deadlines. With these, you will know immediately if you are on track or if you are falling behind. With this knowledge, you can use your creative thinking to prevent similar problems from occurring in the future.

10. Take Action

Finally, take action. While planning is important, what is more important is taking action. It doesn't matter how great your plan is if you don't put it to use, right? So, get after it. You have already developed a sense of urgency with deadlines. The faster you move in the direction of your goals, the more creative you will be, the more energy you will have, and the more you will learn. Most importantly, you will enhance your capacity further so you can achieve even more in the future.

How to Make Non-Biased Decisions

In most case studies, you are given enough information to make decisions, and the answers are textbook examples of human decision-making at its finest. They always present situations in which all the facts are known, and people in the examples are thinking logically. This is the ideal situation, but the reality is often disappointing.

In our everyday lives, we almost always never have enough information, and we have to make decisions in the face of ambiguity, and we also have to deal with our own emotions in the decision-making process. We have to contend with uncertainty, risks, and biases, all of which require us to keep our emotions in check.

Thankfully much work has been done by psychologists to understand the way we think and find out how we can make better decisions. Before we get into it, we need to make one thing clear first: we do not think the same way for each situation. You may make a snappy, spontaneous decision in one case, but then the next decision you make requires you to stop and think for a bit. To make things simple, let's say that there are two processes: fast and slow thinking (System 1 and 2, respectively). Both of these have their own values and drawbacks.

Thinking Fast and Slow

The following concept is derived from the behavioral economist Daniel Kahneman. He proposes a framework consisting of two cognitive systems:

- **System 1:** rapid-fire and automatic, this thinking system allows us to make quick decisions that require little mental resources. This process is prone to error, but best used for mundane decisions.
- **System 2:** slow but accurate, this thinking system allows us to make more complex decisions at the cost of more mental resources.

Knowing which one to use is crucial. System 1, as mentioned, allows you to make quick decisions based on assumptions, so it is best used when you need to decide on insignificant things such as which shoes you want to wear for the day. It is not ideal when you need to make important decisions, however, because you will be subject to biases. This is where System 2 comes in. System 2 is more resource-demanding, as it requires you to gather information, but you can deliberate on more complex problems. In short, to make the most out of your decision-making capacity, you need to know which system to use.

Simple Rules for Better Decision-Making

In light of all this, here are some tips to enhance your decision-making:

Rest or Sleep on It

If a decision is important, the chances are that you still have some time to think about it. You want to be in the best frame of mind when you make such decisions, after all. So, get some rest so you can focus. In this case, System 2 is best. Important decisions should not be made on a whim, and you don't want to make them when you feel tired and stressed out.

Gather the Facts

Other than reserving the time and energy to think clearly, you also want to have enough information at hand. After all, the decisions you will make are only as good as the information you have. For example, suppose that you are looking to buy a smartphone. You did some research, but you only found five bad phones. You can take all day to decide which one of them you want to buy, but you will still end up with a bad phone.

But the thing is, you might not have had enough time to gather complete information. Here, you could use System 1 to compensate because you don't have much choice anyway. Still, I recommend that you avoid getting yourself into such a situation in the first place.

So, gather as much reliable information as possible. There's no such thing as "complete" information anyway.

Stay Open to All Possibilities

When we use System 1, we interpret information differently through assumptions. We tend to jump to conclusions or be biased and give more weight behind the information that supports our biases. So, when you need to make an important decision, make sure that you are not using System 1, and stay open to all facts and possibilities, especially those that you do not want or like.

It will be more challenging or even uncomfortable, but it can help you to avoid making the decisions that may satisfy you at the moment but come back and bite you in the future.

Create Rules

Keep in mind that we are all human, so even the best decision-makers are prone to mistakes. We will get tired, unmotivated, rushed, emotional, and stressed at various times. Moreover, it would take forever to gather all the facts and data and then go through each decision in our daily lives.

As such, when the mind is fresh, effective decision-makers often create simple rules and formulas to help guide them in the right direction, and those rules sometimes extend to high-pressure situations. In doing so, you create a checklist of things to do when you need to make a decision, which helps you to remain as objective as possible, rather than relying on intuitive decision-making.

What does this look like when implemented? Think of when you need to make a grocery list. Consider what you really need to buy and stick to it when you are at the store, rather than just browsing from aisle to aisle, being tempted by all the products on sale and your hunger.

Alternatively, you can try to set an upper limit for a big purchase and stick to it. That way, you can stop yourself from buying expensive things that you may struggle to pay for later, such as a big house or an expensive car.

In short, we are all prone to biased and emotional thinking. To minimize this problem, you want to create rules and systems to help your decision-making process.

10 Mind Hacks to Be a Better Thinker

It actually does not take much to be a better thinker. All you need to do is to implement ten of these mind hacks, and you will immediately see improvements in how you think.

1. Trust your gut feelings: as I've mentioned before, the most significant thing that is going on inside your brain is actually in the unconscious section that is often outside your control. It is actually the unconscious mind that does most of the heavy-lifting because this is what filters information we receive from the outside world and then spits out emotions on the other side; we know this as a "gut feeling," and we've always been taught to trust those. Gut feelings are a cross between logic and emotion, because the subconscious mind only follows the system of belief and past experience. You could say that one could replicate gut feelings in the lab. However, it is part of emotion, because of the output. It does not tell us exactly what is wrong, but it tells us that something is definitely amiss. So do not ignore that unsettling feeling when you are about to do something. Your subconscious mind is trying to tell you something.

2. Never think under pressure: again, save the decision-making for later. You're prone to making bad decisions when you think under pressure. So, you want to make some room for your mind to go over the data and available options. But there will be a time when you need to make decisions quickly and with a great amount of uncertainty. What do you do then? Well, try to detach from the situation to give yourself some breathing room. Even if you cannot give yourself the time to think, you can at least give yourself some space by detaching. That means closing your eyes, taking a step back, and taking a deep breath, which allows you to bring your hectic mind to a halt and restart the thinking process.

3. Consider other views: this is a trick employed by many people in a competitive environment to anticipate their opponent's next move. Basically, when you want to make a play, you take into consideration how other players will react. You can also apply it to understand your opponent's strategy and find ways to counter them. Keep in mind that planning is all about considering what could happen, not what should happen. To do this, simply put yourself into the other person's shoes and think as if you were them. What would you do if you were them? Sun Tzu said that if you know yourself and your enemy, you need not fear the result of a hundred battles.

4. Question your preferences: sometimes, your preferences, such as likes and dislikes can blind you to other options. For example, let's say that you love to buy expensive clothes because you have a belief that expensive stuff tends to have a higher quality than the cheaper counterparts. This belief isn't always wrong, but it certainly has flaws. Sometimes, the price for certain products has spiked because of a simple label. A Supreme tag on your shirt won't make it incredibly durable or longer-lasting than its non-branded counterpart. Even if the shirt itself has a higher quality, it probably won't justify its 1000% increase in price. A higher price does not mean higher quality, let alone how much you will enjoy it. Perhaps the fact that you like buying expensive clothes is your brain playing tricks on you. Remember cognitive dissonance? Since you spent so much money on your clothes, you feel the need to justify the price tag, and so you validate your experience even though it is not true. So, what can you do here? Simply figure out what you really like. In our example, maybe the price tag actually does not matter. What matters is that you like to own many articles of clothing and you can start to buy cheaper ones. That way, you can still be happy and save a lot of money in the long run.

5. Take long showers: a shower is a magical place for a bunch of reasons. For one, you always come out feeling fresher than when you went in. But the real magic is the strange phenomena called "shower thoughts." Some say that these thoughts come to you in the shower because you are detached from the world, and so this creates the space that allows your mind to think clearly and properly. You would be surprised to see how some million-dollar ideas come straight from the shower. Most of your shower thoughts will be outright strange. You may wonder, "Why isn't the plural of the word 'pan,' 'pen' when the plural of 'man' is 'men?'" Numerous studies show that you will get these moments most often when you are not aware that you are thinking of the problem at hand. These moments are often when you are taking a shower or a long walk, but since not as many people go jogging or walking at the park, we attribute the source of such thoughts to the shower. This is because the mind does not experience stress or pressure when you are taking a shower or a long walk. When the mind is not under stress or pressure, it starts to think and solve problems on its own.

6. Be skeptical of your memories: what you remember of a past event may not necessarily be what actually happened. Sure, you might be able to recall the general detail of the past with some accuracy, but the smaller details might be muddled. In fact, the more often you recall the same event, the less accurate it becomes. So, basing your decisions on your memories is a bad idea.

7. Don't multitask: the prefrontal cortex is the part of the brain that is responsible for willpower and thoughts. Unfortunately, for something so important, it does not have a large energy reserve. You can tire it out very quickly. For example, suppose that you have to really push yourself into overdrive when you need to complete a project in a pinch; you will tire the prefrontal cortex out. After that, it will be too drained to maintain your willpower, so you are more likely to make impulsive decisions.

8. Learn from your mistakes: we look at successful people as being like a towering building with a beacon of light at the top. The light represents success, and that is the only thing most people see. What many fail to observe is that the beacon is built on top of countless mistakes. Every successful individual will tell you that the key to success is to learn from your mistakes. Many people do not get far in life because they are afraid of making mistakes, but that is the only way to learn and improve. You get a little wiser every time you fail. So be willing to make mistakes and learn from them. Even when you get something right, I suggest that you still look at your performance to see where you can improve. This perfectionism can be unhealthy if overdone, so instead of trying to achieve perfection, settle for incremental improvements instead.

9. Daydream, seriously: daydreaming puts your creative mind to work. Sometimes, you cannot see a solution to a problem until you start to think creatively. Your mind may be muddled already when you try desperately to solve the problem, so you might want to step back and daydream a little to let the logical mind rest and the creative mind work.

10. Think about thinking: think of your own mind as a Swiss Army Knife. It has many uses, but it is only valuable if you know how to use it. Experience or intelligence plays a role in determining your judgment, but this does not matter as much as knowing how to use your mind. The creative, emotional mind may compel you to buy that expensive car, but you want to use your rational mind when you look at the loan terms. So, know which mental tool to use that fits the situation at hand.

Critical Thinking Exercise

Critical thinking is like a muscle. It takes constant practice to improve it. Thinking critically is gathering knowledge and experience. How can we keep improving our critical thinking skills? How can we encourage people to continue improving their critical thinking skills for a lifetime?

Improving our critical thinking does not need hours of lesson planning or require special materials. Thinking critically yields many benefits, but you just need to be curious and open-minded.

There is no magical way to improve our critical thinking immediately, and it will take time to practice routinely. Below are some strategies you can employ to help you improve your critical thinking skills in your everyday life.

Don't Waste Time

Have you ever noticed in a moment of time that you waste time and realize you get nothing back from it? Everyone has this experience in their lives, even the people who are good critical thinkers. Thankfully, we can maximize productivity and minimize time wasted on trivial matters. For instance, you can take the time you would spend watching TV to plan your days ahead.

We have arranged some questions that you can use to review how you practice your thinking throughout the day:

- "At what points during the day did I do my best and my worst thinking?"
- "What did I think about today?"
- "Did anything come out of my thinking?"
- "Did I allow negativity to cloud my thoughts?"
- "If I could do the day over again, would I do anything differently? What, and why?"
- "Did anything I did or thought have any benefit toward long-term goals?"
- "If I spent the next ten years thinking the way that I did today, would anything important be achieved?"

Spend time going through all of these questions, or just focus on a few at a time and think about your responses carefully, and record it in your journal. The more that you spend time practicing this, the better you will be, and you will see patterns emerging in your thinking habits.

Learn Something New Every Day

Embracing the idea of a lifetime of learning is all about making the process of learning an ongoing journey. You just need to learn something new that you did not know before, on a daily basis. You can start by asking yourself something you have been curious to know. Is there a question about something that you want to get an answer for? If so, go and chase it. Do not stop until you figure out the answer you are looking for. No matter how simple or unimportant the question might be to other people, do not take this into account. From this practice, you can learn two things at the same time. You can fulfill your intellectual need and you can develop your habit of curiosity.

No Boundaries for Learning

Never ever think that you are too old to learn something new or achieve something amazing. There are a lot of famous people who only accomplished great things when they were "old," so ignore your age and start learning to do something new. There is no age limit for learning, particularly in the process of improving critical thinking skills.

Always Question

Asking questions shows a sign of intelligence in your brain. Asking questions means you are curious to know something more. In today's world, we should always encourage our children to ask questions more to discover possibilities and opportunities. Questions are always good, and good questions are always better. The core of critical thinking and lifelong learning is the ability to ask meaningful questions that can lead to constructive and useful answers. Encouraging people to learn by asking questions as the focus will ensure that our learners do not learn in only one way. It is a highly interactive learning process when we exchange ideas and discuss them by asking questions. As a result, we can develop a habit of curiosity by asking questions to look for other opinions and views, taking nothing for granted.

The following questions are used for improving critical thinking skills. Think of something that someone has just told you and after that, ask yourself the questions below:

Who?
- "Do I know that person?"
- "Is that person in power?"
- "Is it important to know who told me this?"

What?
- "Is it a fact or an opinion?"
- "Are all the facts provided?"
- "Is there anything left out?"

Where?
- "Public or private?"
- "Was I given a chance to respond?"

When?
- "Is there any reason for their opinion?"
- "Are they trying to make someone look good or bad?"

How?
- "Happy, sad, or angry?"
- "Spoken or written?"
- "Could I understand?"

Active Listening

Active listening is really essential in critical thinking as you will have enough information from the speaker, and by paying attention, you will come up with good questions that lead to gaining more information. Some say that you have two ears and a mouth for a good reason. A good leader lets others talk first before expressing his or her own ideas and opinions. According to a study from the University of Missouri, many people are weak listeners. It does not help when there are so many distractions, either. Most people think that listening is an easy thing to do, but it is actually very difficult to do, especially when this means active listening. To be an active listener, we need to make a conscious and concerted effort to hear words being said by the speaker, and more importantly, we have to understand what is being said within their message. Moreover, it is also crucial to understand what the speaker wants or is striving to achieve in the conversation.

Improving Active Listening

Active listening skills, like other communication skills, can be learned, accomplished, and taught.

- **Talk less:** this should be obvious because it is impossible to both talk and listen at the same time. Listen and do not try to talk or think of a reply just yet. Focus on what the speaker is saying to get a clear message. After that, you can respond. That way, you allow the speaker to say all that needs to be said so you can fully understand what they are trying to say.

- **Adopt a listening mode:** keep silent and pay attention to hear what they are saying. Furthermore, keep the environment quiet and comfortably open your mind by engaging in eye contact. At the same time, make sure you are responding appropriately. Active listening is meant to promote respect and understanding. When listening, you gain more information, data, perspective, and insights. Attacking the speaker and putting them down does not help anyone. Of course, that does not mean you should just sit there and nod, either. This brings us to the next point.

- **Respond properly:** be candid, honest, and open in your response and assert your opinions respectfully. When you respond and provide your own opinions, keep in mind that you can sound just as wrong to them as they do to you. Remember what is important in the discussion: reaching an agreement on the best solution. So, it does not matter who is right. What matters here is that a good decision has been made that day. Plus, you are here to take in ideas and knowledge, and the other person is there to share it. You can save the discussion until after the presentation. There is always an opportunity to talk.

- **Make the speaker feel comfortable:** you have to show some gestures or signs of agreement in your listening. If you think that seating makes you both feel comfortable, you can arrange the seats for the conversation. Be aware of the environment in which you are communicating.

- **Avoid distraction:** this means you have to make sure that you keep your phone on silent mode, keep the TV screen or speaker off. If the person you are talking to requests privacy, you can hold the conversation in a private room and close the door.
- **Put your personal prejudice aside:** it is difficult for most people, but we can tackle this issue through learning and practice. Interrupting people is considered rude and a waste of time because it only serves to infuriate the other person and restricts a full understanding of the message. Therefore, allow the speaker to finish each point properly. In some cases, the speaker will pause, offering you the opportunity to ask a question. That is the time to speak. Also, never interrupt a counter-argument.
- **Pay attention to their tone:** the tone of the speaker's words can sometimes enhance the meaning of the words, and sometimes, it can hide the meaning of the words. Make sure that you know the difference.
- **Look for the meaning:** when we listen, we will hear what other people say. That much is clear. But what people speak out loud may not actually be what they are trying to say. What we want to listen to is the meaning behind their words, not the words alone.
- **Look for the subtle signs:** it is true that the most observable form of communication is speech, but that only makes up a very small portion of the entire communication process. Everyone communicates through non-verbal languages and cues such as body language, facial expressions, and tone. Look out for those when you talk to people. You might understand what they are actually trying to say.
- **Provide feedback:** communication is a two-way street. You speak, and you listen. But sometimes, when you listen, you may not fully understand what is being said due to personal biases, beliefs, prejudices, assumptions, et cetera. So, you want to counteract this problem by attempting to understand the message clearly. To do that,

you just have to paraphrase what the speaker said. Put their ideas in your own words and verify with the speaker whether you understand what is being said properly. If you are told that you got it wrong, ask clarifying questions. Other than that, make sure to summarize what the speaker said now and again during the conversation, to make sure that you are still on the same page.

Solve Just the Problem

In this day and age, everyone has too many problems to solve and too little time. You may run into various problems everywhere, be it at the workplace, at home, or while you are out and about. I'm talking about the problems that you cannot just sweep under the rug. Some problems naturally resolve themselves, of course, but it's your problem primarily because it came from your actions or choices, and this type of problem does not just go away on its own. So, you are left with only one option, and that is to tackle all problems one at a time and do your best to prevent any more from occurring in the future.

Take a moment now and look at what is wrong with your life. If you find that there are so many things that you lose count, do not despair. This is a very common thing. Even the people who you think have it all figured out also have too many problems that they would rather not think about. But here's the thing, you won't get anything done unless you start to look at your life, see the problems, and start to work on solving them.

You want to build momentum, so you don't have to tackle the biggest problems straight away. You can just start solving a problem so that you can steadily improve your life.

As Les Brown once wrote, "If you have a problem that either a man or God can solve, then you don't have any problem." What he was trying to say was that we all worry too much about the problems in our lives, let alone looking at them and solving them. It's a scary prospect for many people. The thing is that problems are inevitable. They are an aspect of our lives, and we all need to learn to accept this fact. We can achieve more in life if we embrace them and see them just as another chore to cross off the to-do list. Then and only then can we move on to solve problems with a more positive attitude.

Now, let's take a look at one approach mapped out by authors Richard Paul and Linda Elder. In their approach, you will have a roadmap toward solving a problem you need to face daily.

• You have to state the problem as clearly and precisely as you can.

• You have to understand about your problem and know what you are dealing with, and you also need to put aside the other problems that you have no control over and save time to focus on the problems that you can actually solve.

• You need to figure out the information you need and actively discover it.

• You need to analyze and interpret the information you collect carefully.

• You also need to identify what you can do in the short term and long term. Figure out all the options for action and visualize the most appropriate solution you want to happen.

• You have to evaluate your options, and take into account their pros and cons.

• You have to take up a strategic approach to the problem and follow through with it.

• You need to track your progress as you implement your actions and be ready to review and alter your strategy should the need arise. Plus, your strategy should be flexible enough to allow changes when more information is available to you.

It takes lots of time and practice to improve your critical thinking skills, but you will see a significant improvement when you follow all of these simple activities and systems.

Asking the Right Questions

Critical thinking is about utilizing the information that you have to the best of your ability. As such, it is just as important to gather the right kind of information. One way to do that is either by observation or questioning. Observation can only get you so far as it can only answer some of the most basic questions.

Asking the right questions allows you to understand the situation better and analyze it properly. The best way is to follow the "Starbursting method" by brainstorming and asking these six questions: How, what, where, when, why, and who?

For example, suppose that you are tasked with solving an accessibility problem at your office. There have been complaints about the fact that certain stair placements have made it difficult for people with disabilities to gain access to some areas, particularly the main entrance, as it is slightly elevated, requiring the use of stairs. So, the questions you should ask first are:

- **Who:** who is intended to use the stairs?
- **What:** what is wrong with the stairs? What are the options to solve the problem?
- **How:** how can we implement our options? How can we design access in place of the stairs in a way that disabled people can use?
- **Where:** where will we use these new ideas?
- **When:** when do disabled people use the stairs the most?
- **Why:** why do we need to change the stair design? Why do disabled people have such a bad experience?

Alternatively, you can also use the element of thought to help you identify the right questions. Elements of thoughts reflect how we think about the situation. They include purpose, questions, information, interpretation, concepts, assumptions, implications, and points of view.

- **Purpose:** goals and objectives. The question: what are we trying to solve? What do I want to achieve?
- **Question:** problems and issues. The question: what should I need to ask?
- **Information:** data, facts, observations, experiences. The question: what do I need to know to understand the problem?
- **Interpretation:** conclusions and solutions. The question: how do others come up with different solutions?
- **Concepts:** definitions, theories, laws, principles, and models. The question: what is the main concept of this idea?

- **Assumptions:** presuppositions and axioms. The question: what are we assuming to be true or false without confirming?
- **Implications:** results and consequences. The question: how can we implicate these new ideas?
- **Point of view:** frames of reference, perspectives, orientations. The question: how are the different points of view related to the problem?

The next step, of course, is to answer all the questions without any assumptions or prejudices. Here, you should have a deep understanding of the problem, and you can move forward with the steps needed to find the best solution to the problem. In our example here, the solution included using elevators in places where people with disabilities can easily find and access them, or using sloped platforms to allow wheelchair users to go up and down easily.

How to Sharpen Your Logical Thinking Skills

We all know about Sherlock Holmes and his unparalleled logical thinking skills. Thankfully, this is something that we all can achieve with a little practice.

Of course, maybe a convoluted murder case is out of your league, but at least you can improve your logical thinking skills to a level that makes problem-solving and decision-making much easier. These skills will contribute to your success in your personal and professional life. So, what can you do to sharpen your mind?

Learn the Terminology

Before you start brushing up on your logical thinking skills, it is worth knowing the set of associated terms and become acquainted with them—such as assumption, premise, argument, conclusion, inference, observation, different statements, et cetera. That way, the rest of the journey will be much easier.

Making Logical Conclusions

It does sound strange, but practice makes perfect. You do not need to get yourself into a difficult situation to improve your logical thinking skills. Trying to think in conditional statements and finding causes and consequences of small and insignificant facts is enough. Basically, just identify the premise and conclusion in any conditional statement and establish a link between them.

For example, let us assume that if it is snowing, it is cold outside. So, we have the statement: "If it is snowing, it is cold outside." In a conditional sentence, if the premise is true, then the conclusion is also true. That's it. Just develop this kind of thinking with other things and see if the relationship works between the premise and conclusion.

Play Card Games

There are other ways to make the learning process fun. Why not gather your friends once every week to play a light-hearted card game to stimulate your brain to think quickly and logically? Challenging card games will only dampen the mood and make the learning process arduous. Simple card games help improve your memory, focus, and analytical skills.

You can even incorporate strategy into these games to spice things up. Games such as Crazy Eight or Go Fish are perfect for kids. For adults, games such as Blackjack or Poker work just as well.

Make Math Fun

Okay, math is one of the least fun things in the world for many people, but it is also one of the best exercises to improve your logical thinking skills. You see, math is more than just crunching the numbers. Those who excel in math are actually fluent in logic because the only difference between the two is numbers and letters. Math is logic simplified so everyone can make sense of it.

Thankfully, you do not need to sit and crunch numbers all evening to improve your logical thinking skills. There are plenty of fun ways to work on your math. There are plenty of mental challenges in math games on many websites or mobile phone apps that you can access.

Other math-related games, such as Sudoku, are also engaging and challenging, allowing you to improve your brain's ability to solve real problems faster.

Solve Mysteries and Break Codes

Another way to improve logical thinking is by reading crime stories and detective novels. They require logical thinking from readers, after all. If reading is not your cup of tea, consider watching movies or TV shows in that genre instead. The challenge here is to solve the mystery before the hero of the story does. Of course, there will be plot twists or different interpretations of evidence, so do not be discouraged if it is actually different from what you have imagined. What matters here is you get yourself to think logically.

In this case, you often have many possibilities. Your work here is to eliminate those that are improbable or impossible. Another great brain exercise is breaking codes, which you can find on the Internet and play with your friends.

Debate

Debates challenge us to string our thoughts together in a convincing way. While we know something is good or bad, explaining that to others is difficult. Debates force us to search for causes and consequences behind our beliefs, and turn them into strong arguments and find the logical connection behind everything.

Because you need to think logically and decide on the fly, debates can improve your logical thinking skills. So, join a debate club or organize a debate with your friends about literature, society, music, politics, et cetera.

Be Strategic

Logical thinking is all about understanding logical connections and putting the pieces together. By learning how to think strategically, you will develop a valuable asset for both your personal and professional life. Strategic thinking habits include anticipating, critical thinking, interpreting, deciding, and learning. You can improve this kind of thinking by playing strategic games such as board games, video games, or brain-enhancing games or design a strategy for sports events.

Notice the Pattern

Individuals with great logical thinking skills see patterns that others might otherwise miss every day. Those patterns will put their logical reasoning skills to the test, along with the ways that they anticipate and complete them. A great way to train pattern recognition is by scrutinizing everything and finding an answer through an educated guess.

For example, we have a string of numbers: 1, 4, 9, 16, and 25. Which of the numbers below follows?

a) 50
b) 36
c) 44
d) 78

If you chose "b," then congratulations. You noticed the pattern in the numbers. Each number in the string is squared and goes up by one. So, it's 1x1, 2x2, 3x3, 4x4, and 5x5. You need to familiarize yourself with these problems and be able to quickly think of an answer.

Seven Methods of Critical Thinking

"Thinking is skilled work. It is not true that we are naturally endowed with the ability to think clearly and logically—without learning how, or without practicing." A. E. Mander.

Keep Things Simple

Not everything requires a complicated solution, not even all complicated problems. Sometimes, we explain far too much and just end up losing ourselves and others, even down to forgetting what the original problem or question was. Avoid this by going back to basics, back to the questions asked, to try and solve the problem; questions like:

- "What do you know about this already?"
- "How did you know that?"
- "What are you attempting to show, prove, criticize, et cetera?"
- "What are you missing?"

Question Every Basic Assumption

We can all make fools of ourselves by not questioning those basic assumptions. Most scientific breakthroughs began with a challenge to a commonly held belief—innovators simply ask, "What if I was wrong?" Questioning your assumptions will allow you to think more critically about possibilities and about what is appropriate.

Know and Understand Your Own Mental Processes

Humans can think critically, and that is what puts us above other animals. However, it isn't always easy to think critically, mostly because of how we think. The human brain relies, to a large extent, on mental shortcuts, as a way of explaining things happening around us. While that may be useful when you need to make a very quick decision, it may not be so useful when you are making life-changing decisions. Mental shortcuts are not always the most accurate, and that is why it is so important that we are aware of cognitive biases and personal prejudices, because both can affect our decisions.

Yes, all humans have cognitive biases of some description; it's being aware of this that makes us able to think critically and it is something all critical thinkers must consider.

Reverse Things

If you find yourself deadlocked, unable to solve a sticky issue, reverse things. Yes, we know that X is responsible for Y, but what if it were the other way around; what if Y was responsible for X?

The obvious example is the chicken and the egg. Yes, we know that a chicken comes before the egg; the chicken lays the egg, so that is logical. But what if we were to ask where that chicken came from? Well, a chicken comes from an egg, so, surely, the egg comes first, yes?

At times, you will know immediately that the reverse simply isn't true, but it can put you on the right path for the right solution.

Evaluate the Evidence

One of the most useful things we can do is evaluate previous solutions to similar problems, and it is important to do this critically. If you don't, you can be sure you'll come to the wrong conclusion. Ask yourself a few simple questions—where did the evidence come from? How was it gathered? Why did the other person solve the previous problem in that way?

Take research that was done into sugary cereals, for example. One study, quite persuasively, showed that, in fact, sugary cereals are good for your health. Now, deep down, you know that really isn't true, and when you delve deeper into the evidence, it comes to light that the cereal company paid for the study. In that, it's probably fair to say that that company influenced the study.

However, it would be wrong to write off the result as not being valid; what we should do is keep it in the back of our minds that there may be a conflict of interest.

Think for Yourself

Not everyone has faith in themselves, putting all their trust in reading and research. Often, people forget that they can think for themselves; they forget to use one of the most powerful tools at their disposal—their own minds and brains. Overconfidence is not clever; just understand that, at times, the only way to reach a solution is to think for yourself. Use your own opinions, thoughts, and ideas, and don't just rely solely on other people's.

We Cannot Think Critically All of the Time

It just isn't possible, but you know what? There's nothing wrong with that. Just remember to use critical thinking when it comes to making complex decisions or solving tough problems—you don't have to think critically all of the time and about every single thing.

Six Steps for Effective Critical Thinking

We have to deal with problems on a day-to-day basis, from small and insignificant things to major, life-changing decisions. In many cases, we are challenged to understand a different perspective when we approach any situation. Our thought processes are based on previous experiences or similar situations. While that allows us to think quickly, that does not always mean we can solve problems effectively because our emotions may cloud our judgment. Not only that, our decisions may be further affected by prioritizing the wrong factors, or other external factors as well. Here, critical thinking allows us to establish a rational, open-minded decision-making process that is based mainly on solid facts and evidence.

As we have mentioned earlier, we have developed some mental shortcuts that help us make decisions quicker, especially during life-or-death situations. Here, critical thinking prevents us from jumping straight to conclusions. It may slow down our thought processes, but it helps us to make the right decision. It helps guide us through logical steps that allow us to discover more perspectives and solutions while removing those mental shortcuts that are based on personal biases. The critical thinking process has six steps:

1. Knowledge

Every problem requires a clear vision to see the right solution. In this step, you need to identify the problem. To do so, ask a lot of questions to understand every little thing about the scenario. That way, you can understand what influences the outcome or what you need to address from the start. In some cases, there is no actual problem, so no need to go forward with the other steps. This is just as important, because trying to solve a problem that does not exist is a waste of time and may worsen the situation. To identify the problem, start by asking open-ended questions to gather as much information as possible and pave the way for discussion and explore the problem. The two main questions to be asked are: What is the problem? Why do I need to solve it?

2. Comprehension

After identifying the situation, you can then try to understand the facts and situations that led up to this moment. The information-gathering process should follow any of the research methods that can be changed according to the problem, the type of data available, and the deadline required to solve it.

3. Application

Continuing on from the previous step, this step requires you to connect the dots from the information you gathered to the resources available to solve the problem. You can use mind maps to assist you in analyzing the situation, establishing a connection between it and the core problem, and then determine the best approach to proceed.

4. Analyze

When all the data is collected, and connections have been made between it and the main issues, then the situation is thoroughly assessed to identify: what is really going on; the pros and cons; and challenges to solve the problem. You should focus on the root causes and think of how you can address them in the solution. You can use a cause-effect diagram to help you analyze the problem and its circumstances. The diagram helps you divide the problem from its causes, and to identify and categorize these based on their types and impact on the problem.

5. Synthesis

After the problem is fully analyzed, and all the relevant information is considered, the next step is to decide how to solve the problem and create an action plan. If there is more than one solution, their advantages and drawbacks should be considered. Identify what you need to prioritize to find the best solution in your interest. We recommend you use a SWOT analysis to identify the solution's strengths, weaknesses, opportunities, and threats.

6. Action

The final step is to put your decision into action. Critical thinking also applies in the action phase, and the action should have its own steps. If your action plan is long-term or involves a team, it is worth having an action plan to help you execute your decision properly.

Moreover, your plan should have certain indicators to identify how well the work is going, so you can evaluate your progress and adapt as needed. Of course, your action plan should be clear but flexible.

Other Ways of Improving Critical Thinking

Critical thinking is a process by which we systematically, deliberately if you like, take in information and figure it out for ourselves.

Some of the ways that we can critically consider information include:

- Analyzing

- Conceptualizing
- Evaluating
- Synthesizing

And the information we are thinking critically about can also come from multiple sources such as:

- Communication
- Experience
- Observation
- Reasoning
- Reflection

All of these sources will guide us to have certain beliefs and take action.

Critical thinking is not the way that we regularly think every day. At certain times, we happen to think automatically, but when we think deliberately, we use some of the critical thinking tools and skills to reach a more accurate conclusion.

Most of our thinking every day is not critical, and that's good for us because we do not have to spend a lot of our brain energy thinking about everything. If we had to think about everything critically or deliberately, we would not have any cognitive energy left to think of something else that is more important. Thus, it is good that much of our everyday thinking happens automatically.

However, we can run into problems if we let our automatic mental processes govern important decisions. If we do not think critically, it is easy for people to control us. In our everyday life, if we fail to stop and think deliberately, it is easy for us to get caught in pointless arguments or involved in silly things.

The Six Thinking "Hats"

Your thinking style has its own pros and cons. Optimistic thinkers often see the chances, but tend to overlook risks or downsides associated with them. Cautious thinkers are the opposite, seeing only risks and not opportunities. By changing up your thinking style, you may be able to find new solutions to tricky problems.

The best way to approach a problem is by viewing it from various angles. You can use the "Six Thinking Hats" model to help you adopt different viewpoints. It can also be used as a decision-checking tool in group situations, because you can encourage everyone to explore the situation from many perspectives simultaneously.

By forcing you to move away from your habitual thinking style, the Six Thinking Hats model allows you to look at a situation from a different perspective, allowing you to view it more objectively.

While you can think up a good solution to your problem using a rational, positive viewpoint, it is still worth exploring the problem from other angles. For instance, you can view the problem from an intuitive, creative, emotional, or risk management viewpoint. You may be surprised to see what good solutions you are missing out on. Plus, not deciding based on these viewpoints can mean making a decision that is poorly received by others because their needs are not met, creative ideas are not used, or essential contingency plans are not acknowledged.

Implementing the Six Thinking Hats Model

This model may be used in team meetings, for example, by giving every hat to every person evenly, or individual hats to individual people. In this setting, there is the benefit of preventing confrontation because each person sees the same problem but from a different angle; that means everyone has a valid opinion—each hat is equal to one way of thinking.

White Hat

White hat is a thinking style that primarily focuses on the available data. You look at what information you have, analyze past trends, and try to spot a pattern or learn something from it. Try to find gaps in your knowledge and try to account for them or fill them. You mustn't proceed further than comprehending the facts and knowledge gap. The questions here are: "What do we know?" and "What data do we have?"

Red Hat

Red hat focuses more on intuition, gut feeling, and emotion. The objective of this thinking style is to understand the emotional reaction from everyone without trying to understand the reason behind those reactions. Most importantly, try to understand the responses coming from those who do not understand your reasoning. Here, you should ask, "What do you feel about this suggestion?" and "Does anything feel off for you?"

Black Hat

Black hat is more about what negativity can come from a decision. Everything must be looked at from a defensive or cautious standpoint; rather than seeing the way it can work, look at where it won't work, where things can go wrong. Critically, this type of thinking can show where a plan has weak points, giving you the option of elimination, making changes, or having a plan in place to counter the negative outcomes.

With black hat thinking, your plan can be more solid, because you will see the risks and the flaws before implementation. By the time you implement the plan, it would be too late; resources will have been expended, and you will be too far in to get out unscathed. Lots of highly successful people exhibit over-optimism, and this leaves them wide open because they do not see the issues ahead of them. They are not prepared for anything to go wrong. Ask yourself, "Is there a way for this to go wrong?" and "What risks are there?"

Yellow Hat

Yellow hat thinking is positive, sunny thinking, represented by the color of hope. Optimism helps you to find the benefits in your decisions, to see what values they hold. This type of thinking is motivating, especially when the going is hard. You should ask yourself, "What advantages does this solution hold?" and "Why is this solution a viable one?"

Green Hat
Green is the color of intelligence, and it is representative of a creative streak. With this hat, your approaches to a problem should be creative, promoting free-thinking and little chance of criticism.

Blue Hat
This style of thinking focuses mainly on process control. It is intended to guide the whole decision-making process and determine which "thinking hat" everyone should use. So, when things go wrong, the blue hat will be used to go through the entire process to diagnose what is going on and then apply the correct thinking hat to solve that problem. If it finds that the problem is the lack of ideas, then the green hat will be used. If you find that things go wrong and contingency plans need to be created, the black hat will be used.

An Example of Six Hats
So, how does it look when the six thinking hats are used? Of course, not all of them are needed in most scenarios and which hat you use depends on the aim of the decision. This thinking model can also be used in another context. For example, it can be used to help students develop their creative thinking skills and learn how to identify solutions after they have developed an in-depth understanding of the problem.

To illustrate how these hats would be used, I will give you two scenarios. In the first scenario, different people in the team will utilize different thinking hats to make a decision. In the second scenario, everyone puts their minds together under the same thinking hat but then switches the hat as they go through the decision-making process.

Scenario 1
So, in the first scenario, suppose that you are one of the directors of a property company. The board is considering whether they should invest in a new office block. Preliminary research shows that the economy is flourishing, and there is also a high demand for office spaces because they are being bought left, right, and center. So how would the six thinking hats be utilized in this situation?

Let's start with the white hat. Here, some directors look at all the data they have. In this case, they look at their supply, which is the vacant office space available in the city. Due to the economy, they see that the vacant office space is already starting to go down. If they decide to get the new office building now, then by the time it is built, the supply will be extremely low. Other than that, they also see that the economy is growing, and they expect the growth to continue.

Next, some other directors put on the red hat and look at the current building design. They say that the current design looks dull and does not inspire creativity and productivity, and also point out that the company's previous customers made the same complaints, as well as the fact that the competitors are also switching up their design to something more modern.

Then the black hat thinkers come into play. Here, they look at the economic forecast, and they know that it can be wrong. What if the economy were to experience a downturn suddenly, then all the office buildings would just sit there rotting away, or be only partly occupied for a short while, which means no profit. If that happens at any point in the future, then everyone is looking at an economy with high supply and low demand.

On the other hand, the yellow hat thinkers understand that there are always risks associated with any investment. It will be a huge money sink, but they are more optimistic about the economy. If it is still flourishing and the forecast is correct, then they stand to get a high return on investment. They also acknowledge the danger of an economic downturn, but they suggest various contingency plans to counteract this effect. They can sell the office buildings before that happens or continue to rent them out but on longer-term leases that could last through any recession. This makes renting the office space a very appealing prospect for many businesses, even if the buildings themselves aren't aesthetically pleasing.

Next, the green hat thinkers take the advice from the red, yellow, and black hat thinkers and consider whether they should redesign the building. They have a few ideas here. They can go for the prestige design that looks so appealing that people would still want to rent the space even during the economic downturn, even if it means spending more on the construction. Alternatively, they can take advantage of the recession as the office building costs would go down. Then, they can simply buy out those properties, sell or rent them out after the recession, both of which would yield a high return on investment.

Throughout the process, the blue hat thinkers control how the discussion goes and ensure that ideas continue to flow and encourage other directors to change their thinking hat models and see if they can come up with more ideas.

When you put all of these thinking styles together, the board of directors has a much clearer idea of the situation and its possible outcomes and can make decisions accordingly.

Scenario 2

This time, you are in a group of designers who are tasked to redesign your company's product package. The flow then would be something like this:

First, everyone puts on the white thinking hat to discuss what they know about the package. What does it look like? How do our competitors design their packages? What do the customers say about our package? How well-received are the packages of our competitors?

Then, everyone proceeds to the yellow hat thinking to identify the advantages of redesigning the package, its process, and how the product can benefit from the new design. So, you can ask about the benefits of the redesign or what positive impacts would the new design bring.

From there, the whole team puts on the black thinking hat and looks at the disadvantages of the design change. They discuss the negative impacts on product sales and marketing targets. Here, everyone looks at the risks associated with the design change.

Everyone then proceeds to the red hat thinking, reflecting their emotional reactions toward the current package and the new one. How does everyone feel about the current package? How does it compare to the new one? What might the customers feel toward the new design? How does the team feel about changing the current design?

In the green hat thinking phase, everyone starts to think of the new design from a creative and innovative perspective. This helps the team think about the new design, and they can improve upon the previous one by looking at its design flaws.

Throughout the entire decision-making process, the moderators wear the blue hat to keep the ideas and discussion going and direct it in a way to facilitate the session.

As you can see, the Six Thinking Hats model allows us to view a situation from various standpoints, giving us the chance to analyze the situation further to gain an in-depth understanding. Moreover, this model also provides us with a systematic thinking method by covering the topic from different approaches. This kind of organized thinking can lead you to an ideal solution in the decision-making process.

Conclusion

Thank you for reading *Cognitive Biases: A Fascinating Look into Human Psychology and What You Can Do to Avoid Cognitive Dissonance, Improve Your Problem-Solving Skills, and Make Better Decisions*. With all of the knowledge acquired from this book, you are well on your way to improving your thinking skills and identifying your own biases, and hopefully, learning to be a little less prejudiced.

The key here is to think systematically and go slow if you must. It is always better to think slowly rather than to decide incorrectly. Having good critical thinking skills puts you way above others professionally and personally, as you can decide and act in a way that best benefits everyone. One cannot stress how important it is to develop your critical thinking skills, especially in this day and age, where manipulation and misinformation run rampant.

Thankfully, you are no longer a victim of these falsehoods. Your life will be significantly improved thanks to your new way of thinking. Pat yourself on the back for reading this far, and good luck on your journey.

Resources

Part 1:

https://www.verywellmind.com/lesson-three-brain-and-behavior-2795291

https://www.sciencedaily.com/releases/2018/11/181108142443.htm

https://opentextbc.ca/introductiontopsychology/chapter/3-2-our-brains-control-our-thoughts-feelings-and-behavior/

https://www.huffpost.com/entry/20-psychological-studies-_n_4098779

https://www.mindful.org/mind-vs-brain/

https://en.wikipedia.org/wiki/Heuristic

https://examples.yourdictionary.com/examples-of-heuristics.html

Part 2:

https://en.wikipedia.org/wiki/List_of_cognitive_biases

https://en.wikipedia.org/wiki/List_of_fallacies

https://blog.hubspot.com/marketing/common-logical-fallacies

https://www.boardofinnovation.com/blog/16-cognitive-biases-that-kill-innovative-thinking/

https://www.inc.com/jessica-stillman/6-cognitive-biases-that-are-messing-up-your-decision-making.html

https://www.randstad.ca/employers/workplace-insights/women-in-the-workplace/how-to-subvert-unconscious-biases-at-work/

https://hbrascend.org/topics/how-to-manage-biased-people/

https://blog.iii.ie/inside-track/5-ways-to-reduce-unconscious-bias-in-the-workplace
https://greatergood.berkeley.edu/article/item/how_adults_communicate_bias_to_children
https://www.newsweek.com/parenting-parents-mom-dad-biased-favorite-child-research-study-finances-equal-677768
https://mcc.gse.harvard.edu/resources-for-families/5-tips-for-preventing-and-reducing-gender-bias
https://www.forbes.com/sites/pragyaagarwaleurope/2018/12/03/unconscious-bias-how-it-affects-us-more-than-we-know/
https://www.thoughtco.com/gender-bias-4140418
https://www.sciencenewsforstudents.org/article/think-youre-not-biased-think-again
https://www.theguardian.com/women-in-leadership/2015/dec/14/recognise-overcome-unconscious-bias
https://www.psychologytoday.com/us/blog/in-practice/201508/6-ways-overcome-your-biases-good
https://www.fastcompany.com/90303107/how-to-become-a-less-biased-version-of-yourself
https://hbr.org/2015/05/outsmart-your-own-biases

Part 3:
https://www.verywellmind.com/what-is-cognitive-dissonance-2795012
https://www.drnorthrup.com/4-ways-to-reduce-cognitive-dissonance/
https://en.wikipedia.org/wiki/Neuroplasticity
https://www.designorate.com/steps-effective-critical-thinking/
https://highexistence.com/its-all-in-your-head-how-to-take-advantage-of-neuroplasticity/
https://collegeinfogeek.com/improve-critical-thinking-skills/
http://www.skilledatlife.com/how-beliefs-are-formed-and-how-to-change-them/
https://www.briantracy.com/blog/personal-success/10-step-process-to-solve-any-problem-critical-thinking/
https://www.forbes.com/sites/forbescoachescouncil/2018/10/09/overcome-biases-and-blind-spots-in-decision-making/

https://www.psychologytoday.com/us/blog/persuasion-bias-and-choice/201806/5-tips-better-decision-making
https://www.realsimple.com/work-life/life-strategies/10-ways-better-thinker
https://www.mindtools.com/pages/article/newTED_07.htm

Here's another book by Jerrell Forman that you might be interested in

Printed in Great Britain
by Amazon